The Southern Railway's Withered Arm

A VIEW FROM THE PAST

STEPHEN AUSTIN

Ian Allan PUBLISHING

Title page:
The lush countryside of the North Devon line is captured in this view of Morchard Road station, looking north. Apart from the removal of the loop and sidings, the scene hardly changed over the years. *IAL*

Below:
Postwar changes; 'West Country' class engines arrived in large numbers and on 20 June 1949, *Braunton*, previously No 21C146, is shown with nameplates and BR number 34046. At the front they have fitted a numberplate in place of the circular 'Southern' plate, but have not removed the painted number S21C146, which was applied in the first month of Nationalisation in 1948. The BR lion emblem was not yet in production. Behind her, one of the new standard sets of Bulleid coaches forms the 2.10pm Ilfracombe-Exeter. This same locomotive returned to reside on the shore of the Bristol Channel nearly 50 years later. *S. C. Nash*

Dedication
For Mrs Rowe of Padstow

First published 1998

ISBN 0 7110 2622 X

Published by Ian Allan Publishing

an imprint of Ian Allan Publishing Ltd, Terminal House, Station Approach, Shepperton, Surrey TW17 8AS.
Printed by Ian Allan Printing Ltd, Riverdene Business Park, Molesey Road, Hersham, Surrey KT12 4RG.

Code: 9811/B1

Front cover, top: Ivatt '2MT' No 41313 heads south alongside the River Taw with the Torrington train in May 1960. *Colour Rail*

Front cover, inset: Drummond 'T9' No 30715 crosses the viaduct over Little Petherick Creek on its way to Padstow in September 1959. *Colour Rail/Derek Cross*

Front cover, poster: BR era promoting Ilfracombe. *Author's collection*

Back cover, top: Beattie '0298' No 30585 crossing the main road on the route to Wenford Bridge in July 1961. *Colour Rail/Peter W. Gray*

Back cover, centre: 'Battle of Britain' No 34078 *222 Squadron* draws in to Camelford station with the up 'Atlantic Coast Express' in April 1964. *Colour Rail/P. A. Fry*

Back cover, poster: SR era promoting 'Go as you please tickets'. *Author's collection*

Contents

Right:
The North Devon line diverged from the Bristol & Exeter main line at the Cowley Bridge Inn, at the north end of Exeter. The signalbox perched beside the River Exe, which at this point had two channels. Here an up goods of 23 wagons comes across the bridges on 26 August 1946. The engine is 'L11' class 4-4-0 No 409, built at Nine Elms in June 1906 and scrapped in June 1951. This engine spent the first half of her career at Nine Elms and the second half in the West Country. No 406 of this class had the sombre distinction of hauling into Exeter in 1936 the only item of Lynton & Barnstaple stock not scrapped on site: the engine *Lew*, exported to Brazil.
B. A. Butt

Foreword

The purpose of this volume is to give an airing to some photographs of those railways west of Exeter which became part of the Southern Railway; to introduce the system to anyone who does not yet know it; and to help the rest of us to sit back and, in our minds, potter about our favourite places with the aid of some views from the past.

'From the past' it has to be, for those railways no longer exist. We are not forgetting that at present one can ride on a train from Exeter to Barnstaple Junction or Okehampton, and from Plymouth to Bere Alston and Gunnislake. However, a single length of plain track on which a diesel railcar shuttles to and fro picking up passengers from car-stops is not, with all respect, what we mean by a railway. To us, every station should have a house, booking office, lock-up, goods shed, coal office, lamp room and signalbox; and trains should be willing and able to deliver everything the people want from a handkerchief to a harvester.

This group of railways fanned out from Exeter Queen Street (later renamed Central) to Ilfracombe, Torrington, Bude, Padstow, Bodmin, Callington and Plymouth, with branches to Lynton, Ruthern Bridge, Wenford Bridge, Cattedown and Turnchapel: about 265 miles in total. They all came under the influence of the London & South Western Railway and in most cases that company supplied the trains which ran on them. Thus, they were, in effect, a unified system before the creation of the railway 'Groups' in 1923.

The 'Withered Arm' is the nickname under which these lines are widely known, but it does not do them justice and is certainly not a fitting image by which they should be remembered. Sometimes attributed to the Southern Railway management of the 1930s, it presumably reflects the attitude of the protagonists of 'Southern Electric' to these rural properties. It is true that they did not yield great profits; but they were well run by dedicated railwaymen who served a large tract of country as well as their circumstances allowed.

The business divided into local traffic, and that from England beyond Exeter. The former was of course the weaker part. People might use the train to go shopping to Barnstaple, Tavistock, Plymouth or Exeter, if it suited them, but with a widely diffused population it would not suit many. The most regular passengers were the tidal flows of schoolchildren. Workers in the remotely situated Marland clay works were carried in by train. For a few years from about 1900 there was a lively commuter traffic in the Plymouth area, but after World War 1 the populace decided they preferred buses.

Within the area, local trains worked from Barnstaple to Ilfracombe and Torrington, Okehampton to Bude and Padstow, Padstow to Bodmin, and Plymouth to Tavistock or Brentor. (Why Brentor, in the middle of nowhere? You've guessed it — a director lived there.) To handle local work, modest depots for the servicing of coaches and engines operated at Barnstaple, Wadebridge and Plymouth. Stabling points at Okehampton, Torrington, Bude and Callington were used for most of the history of the lines; others such as Holsworthy or Delabole had short service as the system developed.

The chief benefit to most people from the railways was cheap coal. It was shipped in, principally to Fremington, for distribution, and every station had a coal merchant. Everyone needed it for heat, light and power, either directly or indirectly in the form of gas. The railways used it, of course, and so did ships: steam trawlers working out of Padstow, for instance. There were a few other mineral flows: sea sand, and clay from Wenford works to Fremington or Fowey for export. Farm produce was taken from rural stations to the towns. But the main customers were away up country. Vegetables, meat (dead and alive), fruit, milk, fish, flowers; every day one or two freight trains made their way up each line picking up loads, and passenger trains acquired tails of vans. Gathered up in yards at Halwill, Okehampton and Yeoford, where shunting engines were usually at work, they reached Exeter, whence not less than three, often more, express goods trains set out every night for the long haul up the main line. Cattle breeders sent train-loads all over the country. Slaughterhouses operated in every town. At Halwill, Holsworthy and Camelford they adjoined the railway; carcasses went straight into containers which went up to Nine Elms and the meat was in the London markets next morning. And one should not forget the railway itself as customer. Its own quarry at Meldon supplied stone for building work and track ballast, sent out daily to all parts of the system.

Coming the other way, great importance was attached to the newspaper train. Starting from Waterloo between 1am and 1.30am and running express to Exeter, it conveyed vans for 11 final

Below:
On the evening of 17 May 1962 'West Country' No 34033 *Chard* rounds Dennis Cove on the way in to Padstow. She is hauling only one coach on the 6.13pm from Wadebridge, a return trip which was carried out by the engine which brought in the down 'Atlantic Coast Express'. In the background is Little Petherick Creek Bridge, and above, the Jubilee Obelisk on Dennis Hill. *S. C. Nash*

destinations. The precious words of wisdom that screamed off the London presses each night were put out in bundles all the way down until the last of them reached Padstow at about 10 o'clock. During the rest of the day the empty vans were collected up by a variety of trains to make a less hurried return to London.

From their inception, all the main routes had through passenger services to and from London, three or more a day. As Bodmin, Callington and Turnchapel did not share this benefit, one suspects that the lure was not so much access to the commercial and cultural prospects of London as the harvesting of a lucrative crop of tourists. Be that as it may, at most stations you could step into a carriage and step out of it at Waterloo; or, more to the point for most folk, you could escape London at nine in the morning and be in Bideford by half-past three. On Friday nights in the high summer season you could even have dinner at Waterloo and breakfast in Padstow. This philosophy contrasted with the behaviour of certain other railways where the expresses were very fast but

the wayside stations and branches were only served by desultory connections. Through carriages ran between London and Exeter as combined trains; then they divided up at Exeter, Barnstaple Junction, Okehampton and Halwill to fetch up in Ilfracombe, Torrington, Bude, Padstow and Plymouth. Later, or usually next day, they reversed the procedure to end up coupled together again at Waterloo. These trains were, in general, hauled by the engines which worked the overnight freights.

Another consequence of the through-carriage principle was that the popular picture of country travellers lumbered with antique rolling stock in which even the fleas had beards did not apply here. Current LSWR stock found its way west — eight-wheelers; the new elliptical-roof coaches of Surrey Warner; steel-bodies ('ironclads'); Maunsells; then Bulleids — and even if local trains did not get the newest coaches they were only one generation behind.

The long-distance traffic was operated from Exeter. At Exmouth Junction were storage and repair facilities for locomotives and wagons, and coaching stock was handled at Queen Street station (renamed Central in 1933). Then, of course, there were the men who ran the trains. The South Western was by far the biggest employer in the town; and since

railwaymen as a group are more public-spirited than most, it exerted a profound influence on the life of the town overall. In the summer season, when everything with wheels was needed on the road, operating staff went out on temporary assignment to the outlying stations, their places being taken by men from further up country. If you worked on the railway, these transfers were the nearest thing you got to a summer holiday.

The relationship between the railways and their public in this part of the world was not cosy. The company claimed, with the unassailable argument of figures, that the people, who had agitated so vehemently for lines to be built, did not use them as much as they had promised they would. After World War 1 they were kept afloat by income diverted, for the sake of goodwill, from the Southern Electric services, and by Government subsidies. The people claimed that services were inadequate and not in tune with local needs. What else could you expect, they said, when the system was managed by a bunch of city slickers in far-off London? The company was not wholly to blame; it did invest, especially in the period around 1930, relaying track, lengthening platforms and adding sidings. But when a train collected only a handful of passengers, the

Left:
LSWR 'O2' class engine No 200, running as BR No 30200 in about 1950, on a Padstow-Bodmin train, starting away from Dunmere Halt. The halt shelter is partly visible beneath the bridge, which carries the main Bodmin-Wadebridge road. The coaches are a Maunsell Composite and brake composite. *L&G*

shareholders wanted more than blind faith in the belief that if an extra train was produced enough passengers would materialise to fill both of them. Nor could you blame all the people; the resident population of the countryside diminished throughout the life of the railways, and rural employment declined faster. If a demobilised soldier who had been given a surplus army lorry turned up at your gate and offered to undercut the railway rate, you would have had to be uncommonly public-spirited to refuse. More of the remaining people were incomers with money enough to retire to the countryside, and of course they could afford to run cars.

But efficiency is not everything in a good life, and what makes this system so popular is that its individuality and its human scale were not improved out of existence. It was never straightened out and strung with overhead wires. Its station houses were not replaced by multi-storey car parks with concrete-slab booking offices. It did not become a humming gadget. Its gates clanged, its signal-wires swished, and its trains puffed.

The other great virtue of the 'Withered Arm' is of course its glorious setting. It is beyond doubt that the way to bring large numbers of people into beautiful countryside without destroying the very beauty that attracted them is to use railways. In the great holiday booms of the 1900s, the 1930s and the 1950s the potential of the lines in this respect was pretty well fully utilised. The single coach became a train of 10 and if that was not enough another one was turned out. And it was all done without cutting down one extra tree. No load of fish or fertiliser ever knocked down a touring cyclist or scared any elderly lady trying to cross the road to the shops. The way these railways threaded their

way through the countryside is an object-lesson in how people may live and work in a nice place without smashing it to pieces. Fortunately, we still have pictures to show how it was done.

Post-Steam
Come Petrol, spirit of the traveller's joy:
Whereas my forebears packed their trunks
And settled to a porter's salute to journey,
I load my own magic carpet, self-piloted,
And once more it's the open road for me.
And those deadly twins, Free Choice and
    Market Forces
Regard the silent strip of weedy ground
That once led down to Cornwall. Still, we find
Each field and weather-moulded tree and hedge
Welcoming us, who now come down by car.
The empty trackway, wind in the willow-herb,
Winds up from Egloskerry to Tresmeer
Through indifferent and encroaching fields,
Past farms whose sons await with eagerness
Their motorway link. Could it really have been
That this same steel road came from Waterloo?
Past Wadebridge station, what a breath of steam
Scents the Camel Valley in our thoughts, as there
It lingers, in a quietness of its own, amidst the
    noise.

S. H. Austin (after Betjeman)

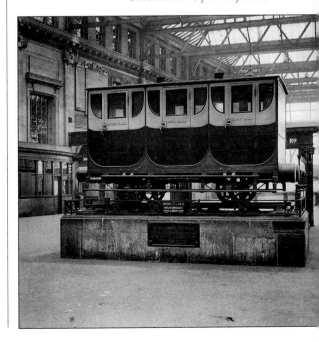

Right:
This Bodmin & Wenford Railway first/second-class coach was placed on a plinth in the new concourse of Waterloo station. The plate reads 'Original coach and permanent way used on the Bodmin & Wadebridge branch from 1834 to 1886'. Above it is a donation box for the LSWR Servants Orphanage and Widows & Orphans Funds. This shows the coach after it was overhauled for the 1925 Stockton & Darlington Centenary celebration. *Southern Railway*

Above:
A view over the Wadebridge headquarters of the B&W before it was rebuilt in the 1880s. The camera is on the north side of the River Camel, looking south. The valley to the left is formed by the Treguddick Brook which flows down from St Breock Downs and under the road bridge. In the yard are five wagons on the sand siding, and just above the foreground building are the four posts of the lift bridge which carries the siding over the brook. The biggest building is the new Town Hall, sponsored (as you might have guessed) by the Molesworths. *L&G*

Below:
The head office of the B&W was the little square building complete with a clock and weather-vane, essential adjuncts to railway operation. In front of it a siding goes through the gate and across Molesworth Street to quays for transhipment of freight brought up by ships which could not pass the bridge. On the far bank of the river are the sheds of Wadebridge's shipbuilding industry. This view was taken in the period 1882-7. *L&G*

1. Bodmin & Wadebridge

If you alighted from the train at Wadebridge station, or came on foot or by car across the long bridge over the River Camel, you entered upon Molesworth Street, the main street of the town, rising from the river bank. The Molesworths were the great landowners of the district, and in the year 1831 Sir William Molesworth resolved to make his estates more prosperous by bringing in the latest technology. In this he was following the example set by the Earl of Stanhope with his Bude Canal to the north and Joseph Austen Treffry with his canals and tramways to the south. He proposed a railway from Wadebridge up the Camel Valley. This was not the first railway proposal in North Cornwall, for the Duke of Northumberland had mentioned building one from Polson on the River Tamar to Launceston, and in 1825 that itinerant enthusiast William James suggested a Padstow-Fowey railway; however, those were not serious proposals, whereas Sir William's definitely was. He engaged Roger Hopkins to engineer the railway and, after receiving an Act of Parliament of 23 May 1832, they had the line open from Wadebridge to Bodmin on 4 July 1834. The rest of the main line to Wenford Bridge and a branch to Ruthern Bridge were opened on 30 September. Passenger services normally ran only between Wadebridge and Bodmin, but the opening train went up to Wenford. In the excitement there was talk of extending the line round Bodmin Moor to Launceston and even to Exeter!

The B&W was not the first railway in Cornwall — that distinction belonged to the Redruth & Chasewater — but it was a pioneering concern in several other respects. It was the first railway in southern England designed to be worked throughout by locomotives, and was the second standard-gauge line in the south. It carried passengers from the start and, long before Thomas Cook,

ran excursions in connection with local events. It had its own workshops, well enough equipped to build its own coaches. Its principal traffic at first was sea sand carried inland to improve the soil. Only later, in 1862, did it begin bringing china clay down from quarries near Wenford Bridge, business that kept the line going long after it had been forsaken and forgotten by the local people for all other purposes. Farm produce and building stone from local quarries brought useful outward traffic. Quarrying collapsed in the early 1930s and the Ruthern Bridge branch was closed down in November 1933.

The Wadebridge terminus occupied a site by the River Camel between Molesworth Street and the Treguddick Brook, adjoining the long bridge. The brook was used as the entrance to a small dock where sand, brought up from the estuary, was unloaded. A transhipment siding went down to this dock and crossed the brook by an unusual bridge; since the tide comes up past this point, the bridge was a vertical lift span, balanced so that it floated up at high water. Sidings extended to the quays on the downstream side of the Camel bridge. The reason the railway did not go further down was that in those days coasting ships could come up to Wadebridge with the tide.

The track, when built, contained what by later standards were regarded as very sharp curves and abrupt gradients. It closely followed the River Camel, crossing to the north bank below Pendavey, a mile out of Wadebridge, and crossing back again at Dunmere, a mile from Bodmin. From there it followed a tributary into the town centre, and a branch continued up the Camel. As the valley became narrower the curves got sharper and the gradient steeper, until at Wenford Bridge it could reach no farther and stopped. A tramway with a rope-hauled incline extended to the De Lank quarries on the moor.

Above:
An 1886 view across the River Camel towards Egloshayle shows the sand dock siding with the lift bridge in partially raised position, and some 1830s wagons. Also visible is a stack of rails for the track renewal scheme. *LGRP/NRM*

The company's stock was not large and initially numbered four coaches, 40 wagons and only two locomotives. The first was named, appropriately, *Camel*; but the builders, Neath Abbey Ironworks, unaware that 'Camel' is a corruption of the Cornish 'Carnel', meaning 'crooked stream', delivered the second locomotive with nameplates reading *Elephant*. The next generation of locomotives was named more conventionally, *Atlas* and *Pluto*.

It is difficult for us at the end of the 20th century to appreciate the impact of the railway. It was only four years since the first locomotive-hauled passenger service anywhere had begun — the first time ever that an ordinary man could move faster than his two feet could carry him — and here was Bodmin at the leading-edge of progress. There have been transport developments since, but none that caused prices of basic commodities to fall and made whole communities down tools for a celebration. Probably the next comparable shock will only occur when towns are suddenly forced to give up motor-cars and use horses instead.

In 1846 the B&W found itself embroiled in the sordid world of railway company politics when the London & South Western Railway offered to purchase it. The reason was that the new Cornwall Railway company, which was a satellite of the Great Western Railway, was about to receive Parliamentary powers to make just that purchase. At that time the two big companies were backing rival schemes for lines right the way down the southwestern peninsula and the GWR was literally miles ahead in the race. The LSWR deal was quite illegal, for a statutory railway may not change its constitution without Parliamentary authority,

Right:
A train of drop-side wagons shunting at the Bodmin terminus in 1888. This was just after the LSWR had tightened its grip on the B&W, and the wagon in the centre is marked with both its B&W number (65) and LSWR number (8820). The barrels on the ground carry 'Royal Daylight' lighting oil. *L&G*

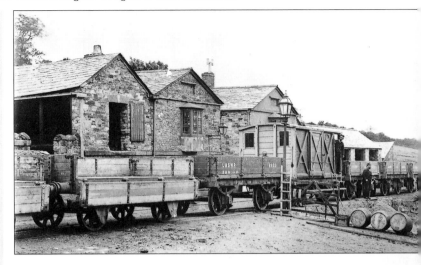

Centre right:
In 1886 some of the B&W coaches were carried off as curiosities and these two were placed on show at Waterloo. Here they are at the east end of Nine Elms Works yard, where a connection went under the main line into the goods station. The solid wooden buffers would have given the occupants a rough ride. *LPC*

Below right:
As a compensation for being exposed to the weather, those in the nearer third-class coach at least had the refinement of a handbrake — more than did the first-and second-class travellers. Contrast the modern coaches behind; but look at the door handles and the curved upper panels. *LPC*

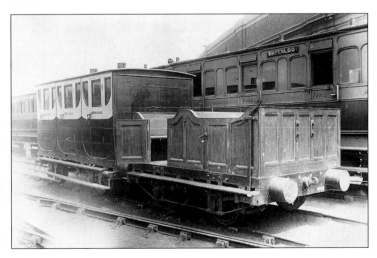

but it was made and went unchallenged until it was approved by an Act obtained in 1886.

The change of ownership made little difference to daily life on the Bodmin & Wadebridge, for it was completely isolated from the rest of the railway system. Such notions as picking up passengers at only designated booking stations were not yet established practice. The first trains had a guard who opened crossing gates, looked out for passengers and took the fares; he also rode on the front of the engine to watch for straying livestock. It was said that the Superintendent usually signalled the train off at one end of the line and drove to the other end to signal it in. As with many a local concern, it was loyally served by an idiosyncratic staff. Typical was Hayes Kyd, Superintendent of the Line from 1861 to 1888. He was an honours graduate of Edinburgh University, a qualified doctor, a Fellow of the Royal Geographical Society, had worked in Australia and was a temperance campaigner. Another known to everyone was Samuel Worth, who joined the railway on its opening and was wharfinger at Bodmin from 1839 until he retired in 1895 at the age of 80.

The railway played an heroic part in the flood of 8 July 1847, which took out most of the Camel bridges and might have taken lives and livestock as well. The train driver, up at Wenford Bridge, saw the storm over the moors and came down the line, sounding his whistle and passing the warning to the inhabitants.

On 3 September 1888 the railway was connected to the outside world, although ironically that link was made by its arch-rival, the Great Western, extending a branch from its own station on the other side of Bodmin to Boscarne Junction, a location a few yards down from the existing junction at Dunmere. Negotiating the agreement for building this link prompted the LSWR management to pay more attention to this far frontier, and they had quite a shock. The effect on sophisticated Londoners was rather like the story by Sir Arthur Conan Doyle, titled *The Lost World*, in which a place was discovered where prehistoric creatures survived; for the B&W, a scientific marvel 60 years earlier, was now an antique curiosity. Their immediate reaction on seeing the state of the line was to stop running passenger trains. Three of its coaches were taken away and preserved, an exceptional action by hard-headed Victorian businessmen.

Improvements were put in hand, including relaying from Boscarne to Wadebridge and straightening the alignment at Grogley Junction and Dunmere Bridge. (One advantage of the slower pace of change in some places is that the original and improved routes can still be seen today.) The termini at Wadebridge and Bodmin were completely rebuilt. These improvements were effected in time for the opening of the link and passenger services were then run through to Wadebridge by the GWR. LSWR passenger trains did not reappear until 1 November 1895. By then they were running into Wadebridge on the North Cornwall Railway, whose completion in the middle of that year finally created an actual pair of rails joining it to its owners in faraway London. The B&W now had three through trains a day to Waterloo and its isolation was well and truly over, but something of its special character persisted for the rest of its life.

After the 1888 rebuilding the railway companies appeared to think they had done enough for Bodmin, once the biggest and most important town in Cornwall. Although the Waterloo express passed five miles to the north and the Paddington express came within three miles to the south, there was never any attempt to provide for direct running into Bodmin. Anyone going anywhere had to change at Wadebridge or at Bodmin Road. Instead of being a focal point of a bustling community, Bodmin North was a sleepy dead-end where nothing much ever happened or was expected to happen.

The section from Dunmere to Wenford Bridge, with its tight curves, steep gradients

Above right:
Most railway vehicles ended up like this one: a B&W van on a typical Cornish farm. The buffers, drawhook and brake handle are still intact. *LPC*

Below right:
Bodmin terminus in its primaeval state, in 1886 before the line was rebuilt. The B&W called its loading points wharves, a reminder of the close relationship between the early railways and the canals. The near wagon is loaded with stone, probably from the De Lank granite quarry. Note, in the track, a modern crossing on the left and a more primitive one on the right. *L&G*

Below:
Road-rail co-ordination at Bodmin Wharf in the 1880s. In front of the tracks is the dock for unloading sand. The Worth family is on parade and Samuel Worth himself is by the wagon on the far right. *LGRP/NRM*

and weight restrictions, remained largely in its primitive condition until final closure on 21 November 1983. Amid the straightening, streamlining and general uglification in which the British delighted, it came to resemble a fantasy from the nation's childhood. At Outlands it cut through a rocky bluff on more a corner than a curve. At Helland Bridge it sneaked between two cottages with barely room for railway vehicles to pass through. Above Poley's Bridge a huge clay processing plant was built and the track beyond it was abandoned in the last few years. As the 20th-century depopulation progressed, this plant was an enclave of noise and dirt in the midst of a silent countryside.

Operating this fantastical railway was appropriately leisurely. The daily working left Wadebridge at 10am. After a protracted spell of shunting at Boscarne Junction to collect wagons which had been worked round from Fowey, the train would move up the quarter-mile to Dunmere Junction, where it would lock into the branch and stand by the cottages between the junction and the main road. The driver and fireman then settled down for 20 minutes while the guard took the point keys back to Boscarne box. Having done that, they were on their own until they reappeared at the junction four hours later. They got back to Wadebridge at half-past

Above:
Bodmin terminus was rebuilt by the LSWR into a fairly conventional station, seen in 1913. On the right is a livestock pen and platform. The single main platform has the usual accoutrements: gas lamps, ambulance box, fire buckets, barrow, etc. The building behind the buffer stops, with a large door and window, appears behind the group of men in the previous picture. *L&G*

four, after a good day's work. You can imagine what the chairman of the new British Railways Board might have said when he found this sort of thing going on in the age of the motorway and the jet airliner.

The LSWR had a problem in powering the branch; since what later generations would call the 'infrastructure' was stuck in the 1880s, the motive power had to match it. Under that policy there arrived in 1893 the first examples of the '298' class 2-4-0T type, displaced from hauling London commuter trains. The last three of these, Nos 298 (later 3298 and 30587), 314 (later 3314 and 30585) and 329 (later 3329 and 30586), became famous among railway enthusiasts all over the country. They arrived at Wadebridge in about 1920, already 45 years old and the last of their type, and were taken out of use at the end of 1962. Throughout this time a succession of railwaymen used one on

Right:
This single LSWR coach standing in Bodmin station probably constituted a complete train; even prior to World War 1 traffic was often light. The wagon to the right is a once common type with a longitudinal bar on top which props a tarpaulin cover and swings to the side for loading. *LPC*

Centre right:
The Bodmin-Padstow service, only needing one coach, was a candidate for the railcar concept. Here is No 8 at Bodmin in 1913. One feels that few stations today would give premier position to an advertisement for the National Gold Medal Suction Gas Pump. *L&G*

Below right:
A view westwards from the buffers at Bodmin, in 1937. In the distance, the massive building with a tower is Bodmin Gaol, conveniently close to the station; executions were a popular spectacle in the early years and the railway ran excursions for them. *L&G*

the branch and one for shunting at Wadebridge, while the third was washing out and was then spare for goods or passenger turns from Padstow to Bodmin, outside which range they never strayed except for visits to Eastleigh for heavy overhauls. They shared the shed at Wadebridge with a couple of 'O2' class engines for the Bodmin trains, a couple of 4-4-0s for North Cornwall turns and the visiting engines from Exeter. This amazing survival was part of the folklore of the line and might have gone on longer, had it not epitomised everything that the British Railways Board, the Ministry of Transport and the Government of the day wished to sweep away once and for all time.

No 298 was handed over to the Science Museum, which put her on display at the Buckfastleigh premises of the Dart Valley Railway Co. No 314 was preserved by the London Railway Preservation Society and became resident at its depot at Quainton Road.

Left:
The original B&W bridge over the River Camel near Pendavey, before it was replaced in the late 1880s. Note the elaborate iron balustrade, on a structure which the public would not see except as a glimpse from the window. *L&G*

Below left:
One of the locomotives discovered when the railway was connected to the outside world was this 0-4-0ST *Bodmin*. She was built by Fletcher, Jennings & Co at the Lowca Works in Whitehaven, and bears a strong family likeness to that company's most famous locomotives, the Tal-y-Llyn Railway duo. This view appears to have been taken at Eastleigh. *L&G*

Above right:
In about the year 1893, Samuel Worth stands proudly with the latest piece of 'high-tech' equipment to arrive on the B&W: Beattie 2-4-0T No 248. *LGRP/NRM*

Right:
This is a well-known scene, taken at Bodmin Wharf during the visit of a group of LSWR directors to the B&W in 1886. The entire passenger rolling stock was assembled to form the train for their tour of inspection, hauled by a Fletcher, Jennings engine. *LGRP/NRM*

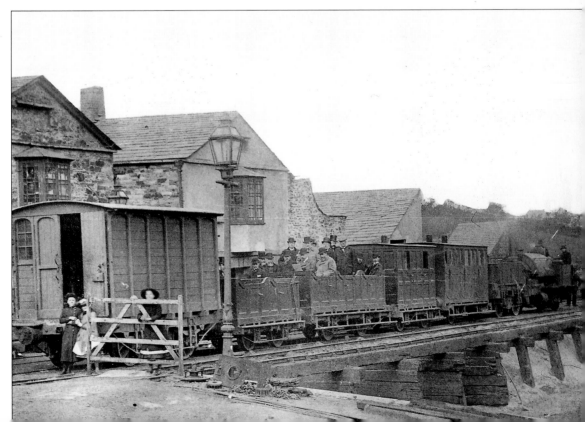

Left:
The 'O2' class engines, designed by William Adams as a small version of the 'T1' class for working both suburban and branch lines, had a long and successful career on the West Country branches. No 200, seen here at Strawberry Hill depot, was built at Nine Elms in 1891. She was in the London area until 1932, then was moved to the west and spent her last 12 years at Wadebridge. She was one of the last to be scrapped, in August 1962. *LPC*

Centre left:
Another 'O2' which had a long career in the West Country was No 183, built at Nine Elms in 1890. She is seen here at Strawberry Hill in 1921, before rustication to Plymouth. She worked on the Turnchapel and Callington branches, as well as on local trains to Tavistock and Brentor on the main line. She finished in September 1961. The pattern on the tank sides is 'Gimp': made by the cleaner with a layer of tallow which he applied on finishing his job. Many cleaners had individual gimp styles. *LPC*

Below left:
After World War 2, No 200 with two LSWR coaches on a Wadebridge-Bodmin service, passing the siding at Nantstallon just before arriving at the halt. The little wooden building houses the lever frame working the points. The engine is far from clean; the headcode disc has not been touched for ages and the smokebox door has been scorched by an accumulation of hot ash inside. *P. Ransome-Wallis*

Above:
Dunmere Halt was a Southern Railway edifice, but
we may assume that trains will have stopped here,
near Dunmere Bridge on the main road, from the
earliest times before the designation of stopping
places. What impresses in this 1947 view is how
immaculate are the permanent way, the grass banks,
the bridge and the platform itself. *LGRP/NRM*

Below:
The original carriage shed and workshop at
Wadebridge looked forlorn in later years,
overshadowed by modern buildings behind them.
This view, taken for their centenary in 1934, shows
the present main line leading to Molesworth Street
crossing. *LGRP/NRM*

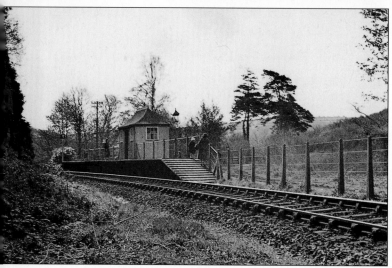

Left:
Grogley Junction, taken in 1934 shortly before closure of the Ruthern Bridge branch, which diverges to the right. The track on the left is the main line, realigned in the 1888 improvements. The siding on the right is on the original route. After it was removed a platform, Grogley Halt, was placed where the camera is. Both main and branch lines eventually became footpaths. *L&G*

Centre left:
Grogley Halt in 1947. Access from the nearby road is by means of the bridge which previously carried the Ruthern Bridge branch line, and is visible beyond the right-hand end of the platform. *LGRP/NRM*

Below left:
Nantstallon Halt in 1937, soon after opening. It has a ground-frame to lock the gates over the road. The fittings are products of the Exmouth Junction concrete factory, whereas the platform shelter is pure Great Western. The large signal just visible is not only to protect the crossing, it is the home signal for Boscarne Junction. *L&G*

Above right:
This view, issued as a postcard in the early 1960s, shows the entire railway installation in Wadebridge. The line enters from top left, past East box by the bend in the river. There are a few wagons in the goods yard; the station is deserted, there is an engine by the coal stage and two more at this end of the shed. Between the brook and the road lie the original B&W station buildings. By the turntable is a stub end of the sand siding, lifted, although the bridge is still intact. Closer to, the quay sidings are crowded with wagons. The main line passes under an SR footbridge and exits bottom right towards Padstow. *RPC*

Right:
Boscarne Junction signalbox, showing signs of neglect in its later years. At this end is the platform where the signalman stands to exchange tablets with the trains. In order to provide a safe walkway to the loops, off to the right, a solid timber deck has been constructed over the rods and wires where they emerge from the front of the lever frame. The mushroom-capped concrete gatepost is a distinctive South Western device, and may be seen today at such places as Venn Gates on the North Cornwall line.
LGRP/NRM

Above:
Seen from aboard a train crossing the road, the fireman of engine No 30200 exchanges single-line tablets with the signalman at Boscarne Junction. Ahead are the passing loops for the two routes, to Bodmin North and Bodmin General. *EWJC*

Below :
Wadebridge means the Beattie Tanks. Here the crew are taking a break during the station shunting turn. No 329 was built by Beyer, Peacock & Co in 1874. This view was taken in 1930, when she had a Drummond boiler and an Adams chimney. Above the number can be seen a letter 'E' (for Eastleigh) indicating that she is an ex-LSWR engine. *L&G*

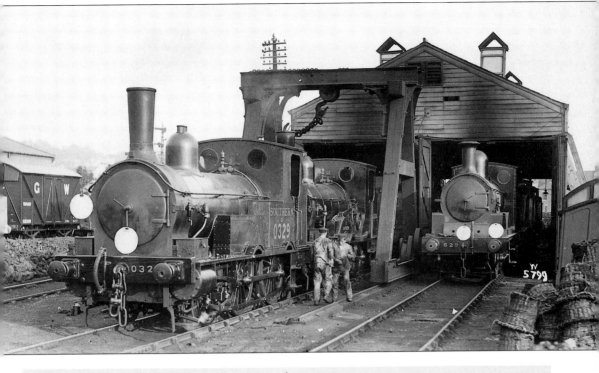

Above:
On Wadebridge shed some time around 1928-30:
No 329 and No 314, built in 1875 also by Beyer,
Peacock & Co, stand while two fitters rush to and
fro, one supposes preparing them for duty. Both
engines are in steam, but the line of engines on the
other road suggests that it might be a Sunday.

On the right is 'Jubilee' 0-4-2 No 629, built by
Neilson in 1893 and destined to be the last of the
class in service at the end of November 1948. Coaling
at Wadebridge was done using wicker baskets of
which some are piled by the track.
RP/NRM

Right:
The same engine, this
time as BR No 30586. She
has now been rebuilt at
the front end, with new
cylinders and a steel
buffer-beam. She is
standing outside
Wadebridge shed, in
front of the lifting gantry.
RPC

Above:
In the late 1950s and still going strong, she passes Wadebridge East Junction, heading for Bodmin with a Southern brake van and a vacuum brake-fitted wagon which has been used for carrying clay. The track on the right is the North Cornwall Railway. *S. C. Nash*

Below:
On 17 May 1962, in the last year of her incredible career, on the beautiful Wenford line. She is heading north along the lower section of the branch where it runs beside the lane leading to Outlands. *S. C. Nash*

2. North Devon

In the northwest corner of Devon, an isolated railway was built to improve the port facilities of Barnstaple. Seagoing ships could not get up the River Taw, but were obliged to stop in the mouth of the River Torridge and discharge their cargo. The Taw Vale Railway & Dock Co was formed in 1838 to build a new port at Fremington and a railway along the south side of the Taw to Barnstaple Bridge. The railway was built to the standard gauge but was a basic affair, the motive power being horses. It began work on 25 April 1848.

The Exeter & Crediton Railway was authorised by Parliament in the year 1845 and in the following year an Act was passed for the Taw Vale Extension Railway, which would extend from Crediton to Fremington (taking over the original Taw Vale line). The latter was heavily backed by the LSWR, while the former was nominally independent but, in fact, the LSWR surreptitiously bought up large numbers of shares.

The Exeter & Crediton was built to the broad gauge, as it connected with the Bristol & Exeter Railway. However, when it was completed in mid-1847, the LSWR used its majority shareholding to have the opening cancelled and the line converted to standard gauge. When that

Below:
The first expresses to Exeter were hauled by the engines designed by Joseph Beattie, such as this, *Argus*, seen at Queen Street station ready to work an up train in the year 1864. She incorporates Beattie's patented coal-burning firebox, and has a plate reminding interested parties of the fact. Many design features are common with the famous 2-4-0Ts. *L&G*

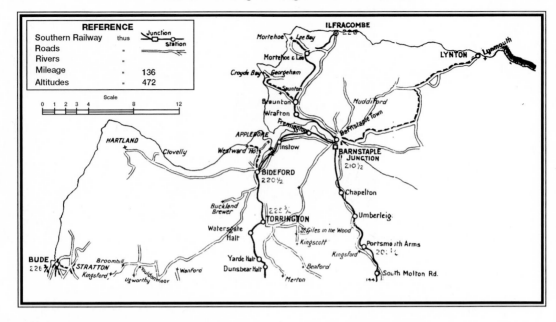

was done, in February 1848 the Government Railway Commission ruled that it was illegal. The LSWR abandoned the entire scheme, leaving the rails to Crediton unused and the Taw Vale Extension abandoned. The Exeter & Crediton company then leased its line to the Bristol & Exeter, which changed it back to broad gauge and opened it on 12 May 1851. That was not the end, however, for the directors were dissatisfied with the management of the B&E, and they placed the lease with the LSWR from the beginning of 1862.

The Taw Vale line, renamed the North Devon Railway and now broad gauge, was built and operated by the contractor Thomas Brassey, who opened it to Barnstaple on 1 August 1854. He rebuilt the Fremington line and extended it to East-the-Water, on the Torridge opposite Bideford, by 2 November 1855. In 1862 Brassey's lease was taken over by the LSWR and the tracks were altered yet again, to mixed gauge, so that standard gauge trains could begin running on 1 March 1863. There was an interim of nine months in which men on the LSWR payroll were using broad gauge rolling stock. Four changes in so fundamental a matter as the track gauge was a record and earned the line the soubriquet in the business of the 'Vicar of Bray Railway'. The broad gauge rails continued in use until the rolling stock was

worn out and broad gauge working ceased north of Crediton in 1877. The Bristol & Exeter, and its successor the Great Western, had running rights and ran a broad gauge goods train to Crediton until the final end of the broad gauge in 1892.

In 1865 a further extension was undertaken from Bideford to Torrington, opened on 18 July 1872. The original Bideford terminus became a goods station. Southwards from Landcross, the tidal limit of the Torridge, this railway took over the line of the Rolle Canal, with a deviation past Weare Gifford where the canal had an inclined plane. The Torrington terminus was actually at Rothern Bridge, over a mile from the town and over 200ft below it. On the face of it this does not appear a logical target for all that expenditure, but railway building was as susceptible as other public works to politics. Torrington was a market town, so it had to be important. It had a canal, so it must be worth serving. There was also the matter of helping the farming of the district. It was axiomatic in the 1860s that better transport brought new life to the remote and underdeveloped, in spite of evidence even then that what it actually did was to suck life out of small places into bigger ones. In practice, most of the passengers got out at Bideford, which was a very cramped station with no room for berthing trains. Torrington,

Right:
A train posed at Crediton station in the period before the broad gauge rails were removed. The complexity of mixed-gauge working is apparent; in front of the Beattie 2-4-0 the narrow gauge crosses from one side of the 'seven-foot' to the other. The Brunel station office on the left survives today. *L&G/EWJC*

Centre right:
Eggesford station house in about 1880; possibly earlier but not much later, as the broad-gauge rails are still in place. An up goods train is drawn up in the platform. The personnel may all be railway staff, but they include a gentleman with a tall hat. *LGRP/NRM*

Below right:
A view of Exeter Queen Street station from New North Road in the early 20th century. The wooded hill on the left is Northernhay, the site of the bailey of Rougemont Castle. A feature of the trackwork is that the point rodding is covered by boards, except in the centre where they have been taken up by fitters. Nearby the driver of 'T3' class 4-4-0 No 574 oils his engine. *L&G/EWJC*

Left:
From the up platform at Queen Street. The original station of 1860 was a single-platform layout of the kind usually associated with the Great Western. The side where the photographer is standing was added some 10 years later. Shunting a four-wheel van and a bogie brake van is 'G6' class 0-6-0T No 259, built at Nine Elms in September 1894 and scrapped in December 1951. A six-coupled tank engine was a rarity on the South Western because of its lack of mineral traffic, the staple of railways everywhere else. Four were based at Exmouth Junction, but none further west until the BR era. *L&G/EWJC*

Centre left:
Queen Street interior in 1913; a very good photograph in such difficult lighting conditions. On the centre road are a bogie passenger brake van and a 'Jubilee' class engine. The refreshment room is offering 'Hot Luncheons 1/6 inclusive 12 till 2.30'. *L&G/EWJC*

Below left:
Passengers boarding a Plymouth-Waterloo express in Queen Street, around 1923-5. The engine is 'N15' class 4-6-0 No 740, built at Eastleigh in March 1919 (later named *Merlin*). *L&G/EWJC*

slightly less cramped, formed a stabling point. Short of amenities Bideford may have been, but you could step from the train into the Royal Hotel without even crossing the street, a luxury denied most major cities.

The stations at Bideford and Barnstaple had in common the situation of being separated from the town by a long bridge over tidal water; attractive in tourism guides perhaps, but unappetising on a stormy winter night if you were late and loaded with parcels. One could blame the town for being on the wrong side of the river, but there it was. The bus went across the bridge and the train didn't. Barnstaple did gain a station on the right side when the Ilfracombe Railway was opened in 1874, when the original station was renamed Barnstaple Junction. To carry that story through, when in 1971 Ilfracombe was shut down, Barnstaple did not consider its Town station, conveniently placed as it was in the centre, to be worth retaining. The railway was cut back to the junction and the few reprobates who wanted to go on using trains had once more to cross the bridge.

On the first day of 1881 a 3ft gauge railway began operating from Torrington to the clay mines in Marland Plain. It was a private line belonging to the Marland Brick & Clay Works

Below:
An up train enters Lapford in 1914. An Adams 4-4-0 is hauling a set of LSWR wooden-bodied bogie coaches. The staff, having been told to look natural, are frozen on the platform: stationmaster, porter, clerk, boy and the signalman holding the tablet. The station house, with roses trained up the walls; posters on the end are 'The South Western Hotel, Southampton', 'Cunard Line, Canada & United States', 'Market Tickets' and a timetable. Not many people from there would go on cruises on the Cunard Line, but a lot of them emigrated on it. (Issued as a postcard by Chapman & Son, Dawlish.) *EWJC*

Top:
All locomotive types were used on all classes of traffic. On 19 May 1952, 'T9' class No 30710 is on a pick-up goods, shunting at Kings Nympton (or South Molton Road, as it had been up to February 1951). The train includes both SR vans and modern steel-ended sliding-door vans. *P. H. Wells*

Above:
An up goods trundles through Umberleigh station on 16 August 1950, the fireman over on the left side of the cab to collect a tablet for the single line. The engine, 'L11' class No 409, has received her BR number, but the tender has not yet been repainted and is still lettered 'Southern'. The 'L11' was a smaller-wheeled version of the 'T9' 'Greyhounds'. The wider-than-standard space between the platforms is an indication that this was once a broad gauge railway. *H. C. Casserley*

Right:
All North Devon trains had to pass through Exeter St David's. Here a Drummond 0-6-0 stands at the middle platform, used by South Western trains, at the head of a train of hopper wagons returning empty to Meldon Quarry. This is No 316, built by Dubs & Co in June 1897, the first of the class to be rebuilt with a superheater in 1920. She was the last of the class and one of the last in service, finishing work in February 1963.
S. J. Rhodes/EWJC

and did not carry passengers, although public goods traffic was taken. It was unofficially known as the Torrington & Marland Railway. There was another minor railway in this corner of the county, the Bideford, Westward Ho! & Appledore. With a title as long as that it was bound to be very minor. The three towns of Bideford, Northam and Appledore were lively places which could have used a good connection, which this was not. It started on Bideford Quay, just below the bridge, and headed due west to the coast, then doubled back and came out below Northam. It opened on 20 May 1901; an extension to Appledore was opened on 1 May 1908. Westward Ho! was a resort built on the hillside overlooking Bideford Bay, named after a novel written by Charles Kingsley while he was staying in the above-mentioned Royal Hotel — hence its unique exclamation mark. Through its short life the railway lost money and the authorities disapproved of it; on Bideford's elegant waterfront it took the guise of a street tramway, and trams were what they had in nasty industrial towns. In 1917 it was abandoned and donated to the wartime scrap drive.

From Cowley Bridge Junction to Crediton the railway was built as a double-track main line, but the rest was single track and became more inadequate as years went by. It was doubled as far as Coleford Junction when the Okehampton Railway was built, and from Coleford to Copplestone and Barnstaple to Umberleigh in

1903, but in 1910 a disgraceful pact was made. The LSWR agreed not to make any improvements to the line if the GWR undertook not to improve its Taunton-Barnstaple line. Thus Barnstaple, the principal and largest town in North Devon and North Somerset, was deprived of adequate railway services; which caused it to turn its interest away from the railways and led ultimately to their virtual disappearance, to the detriment of the entire district.

On the sweeping curves through the broad Creedy Valley from Exeter to Coleford, the line was as much a main line as you could wish; with Plymouth and Ilfracombe expresses (when running as combined trains from and to London they divided at Exeter) and, later, the Pullman 'Devon Belle', there were plenty of impressive trains to grace it. Beyond Copplestone there was a change to a branch-line ambience. The route followed the River Taw as it cut through the high ground of mid-Devon, and as the defile was quite narrow in the neighbourhood of Eggesford Bridge the railway was quite curvaceous, though not excessively so. (Incidentally, Eggesford was home, in 1919, to the first trees planted by the Forestry Commission, an organisation which has attracted so much controversy in rural Britain.) The gradients were good, with nothing worse than the 1 in 125 climb from Yeoford to Copplestone. Fast trains covered the 40 miles from Exeter to Barnstaple in about an hour, which was not bad considering that they had to slow right down at the stations to negotiate the crossing loops and exchange single-line tablets.

By virtue of its leases and acquisitions, the LSWR controlled all the railways that fanned out from the Exeter & Crediton, and they became part of the Southern Railway; but through all this time they were physically separate from the rest of its system. From the Exeter terminus at Queen Street to Cowley Bridge a gap of just under two miles intervened, and in it was the main line of the Bristol & Exeter, part of the Great Western Railway from 1876. By good fortune it was just possible to construct a link line from the west end of Queen Street to the Bristol & Exeter station of St David's. It involved a right-angle bend, a tunnel, a huge embankment and a gradient of 1 in 37; although later exceeded in length in other countries it was and remained the most severe incline on a trunk line in Britain. It was brought into use on 1 February 1862, the day when the LSWR began working the Crediton and North Devon lines and the

day when an agreement enabled it to use the B&E track through St David's to Cowley Bridge Junction. St David's was now the classic traffic bottleneck, as it was the only rail access to the entire country to the west. Co-operation was excellent but the fact remained that the whole of the 'Withered Arm' lay apart from its parent company and could only operate by courtesy of the company's rival. Its trains had to cross over the Great Western's busiest main line, which itself was being worked to capacity in holiday periods. For all that, no-one could face the enormous cost of improving the intersection, until in 1935, with Government money in the offing, work started on an independent Southern station on the west side. A diversionary channel was cut to take the River Exe out of the way, then the scheme was stopped and the site, now an island, is today a public park.

(There was a diversionary route, if you were coming from Taunton. You had to go from there to Barnstaple Victoria Road, round to Barnstaple Junction and back to Coleford Junction.)

Below left:
One of the great institutions was the nightly newspaper train, using bogie vans such as these. They are at the east end of Exeter Queen Street, being shunted into, or out of, the down platform. The shunting engine is 'M7' No 328, one of the 1911 batch built at Eastleigh, and based at Exmouth Junction for many years. *EWJC*

Above right:
Another regular cargo was meat in insulated containers or vans. 'N' class 2-6-0 No 31846 stands in Exeter Central, having come up the bank with four containers from the North Cornwall line. This view was taken on 21 August 1960 and includes one of the last generation of Southern coaches, designed by O. V. S. Bulleid. Above the train is the main building, opened in 1933. Under the footbridge lie the carriage sidings, and a 'West Country' and a 'Z' class engine can be seen. No 31846 was one of the engines built at Woolwich Arsenal in 1920 and bought by the Southern in 1925.
K. A. Stone/EWJC

Centre right:
From 1922 the 'T9' class were rebuilt with superheater boilers and larger cylinders. Here are a cheerful crew on No 730, built by Dubs in 1900, rebuilt in 1927 and scrapped in 1957. They are about to take a freight out of Barnstaple Junction yard on 20 June 1949. The leading wagon has a tarpaulin lashed over it, which probably means the roof is leaking. Behind is the wooden engine shed. *S. C. Nash*

Below right:
Bideford Station in 1913, showing the Royal Hotel's entrance from the up platform. Between the hotel and the platform awnings is a bridge over the road. *LGRP/NRM*

Left:
Instow station in 1913, looking north. On the up side a substantial wall gives some protection from the wind off the beach, which lies on the other side. At the far end is an ordinary signalbox which achieved fame many years later when it became the first such utilitarian structure to be scheduled by the Government as a building of historical and architectural importance. It stands to this day as a focus for the railway revival movement in north Devon. *LGRP/NRM*

Centre left:
Torrington station in 1913, seen from the road bridge — which was not then a bridge as far as the standard gauge line was concerned, as the station was a terminus. A freight train stands in the loop, and another engine is outside the engine shed (the black building behind the platform). The baskets stacked by the lamp-post were used in large numbers for exporting rabbits. Widespread puddles are typical of the climate which makes the West Country so green and bountiful. *LGRP/NRM*

Below left:
Torrington goods yard on 14 August 1935, looking from the station approach road. The presence of three wagons of the London, Midland & Scottish Railway shows how the railways provided countrywide transport in and out of every place no matter how small. *J. Waters*

Above:

A Southern Exeter-Plymouth train approaching Cowley Bridge Junction from the south. The formation is, from the rear: two vans, a corridor third coach, a three-coach set, a bogie parcels van, a 'T9' class 4-4-0 so dirty as to be anonymous, and GWR 2-6-0 No 6387. The vans, carrying meat, livestock and vegetables, were frequently attached to passenger trains. The appearance of GWR engines on the Southern route was quite usual. They had two trips per day over it and the crews were rotated so that they all knew the road and could use it when the GWR sea wall section in south Devon became impassable due to winter storms. *B. A. Butt*

Right:

There were some locomotives named after West Country rivers, but they did not run in the West Country until after they lost the names and were drastically changed in appearance. This is No 806 *River Torridge*, a 'K' class 2-6-4T built at Brighton in 1926 for working expresses on the comparatively short distances in the South-East. In 1928 the class were rebuilt as 2-6-0 tender engines and transferred to the South Western section. No 806 survived to be preserved and now runs on the Mid-Hants Railway. *LPC*

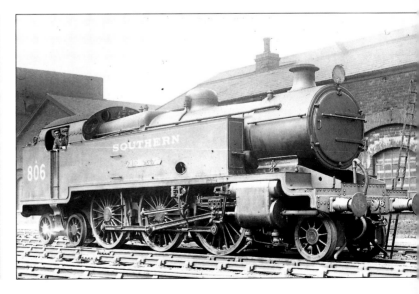

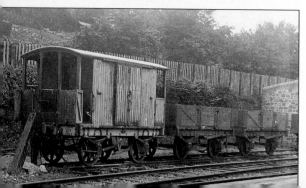

Above left:
This is a Brighton 'Terrier' 'A1' class engine in the heart of the LSWR, at Exeter Queen Street station, the picture featuring the iron railings of the path which made such a splendid grandstand for viewing the activities there. She was built in January 1877 as LBSCR No 46 *Newington*. In 1903 she was one of a pair purchased by the LSWR for working the Lyme Regis branch, numbered by it 734 and 735. This view was probably taken between August 1903 and May 1907; each weekend the branch engine was changed over, the off-duty one being brought back to Exmouth Junction shed for wash-out and examination. After 1907 she was used for odd jobs until being sold to the Freshwater, Yarmouth & Newport Railway in 1913. After Grouping she became No W8 *Freshwater*, and after Nationalisation she was brought back to the mainland and numbered 32646. In 1963 she was preserved and now works on the Isle of Wight again. *EWJC*

Left:
A new shape on the West Country railways: the 'West Country' class engine. On 25 June 1949 No 34007 *Wadebridge* has arrived at Exeter Central with the North Cornwall part of the 'Atlantic Coast Express'. The signal is off for her to draw away with the first coach, provided for passengers to Exeter, leaving the remainder to be combined with the rest of the train for its journey to London. *S. C. Nash*

Left:
The Bideford, Westward Ho! & Appledore Railway station at Westward Ho! was well-appointed, with signalbox, waiting room and store — there was even a penny-in-the-slot weighing machine on the platform. Mind you, the photographer has crouched down to make everything look bigger. This view was taken in 1913. *L&G*

Below left:
Although the BWHO&A Railway was standard gauge, its rolling stock had the central buffer/coupling normally associated with the smaller gauges. In this it could be said to have been ahead of its time, for the 'Buckeye' coupler now widely used is an elaborate version of the same device. *L&G*

3. The Plymouth Main Line

The two great railway interests fighting for business southwestwards from London, the Great Western and London & South Western, pursued their rivalry down the country with a variety of far-fetched schemes. By far the biggest attraction was the port of Plymouth. The LSWR approach to this prize was hesitant and piecemeal. Having obtained control of the North Devon Railway, it backed a quasi-independent Okehampton Railway, incorporated in 1862 to build a line to that town from Coleford Junction. The objective clearly was not Okehampton, for within a year the company had changed its name to the Devon & Cornwall Railway and had obtained authority to extend to Lidford (later renamed Lydford). There it would meet the broad gauge Launceston & South Devon Railway, and the latter agreed to convert to mixed gauge so that trains could run through to Plymouth.

However, lack of funds and the mountainous terrain made construction very slow. The line was opened to North Tawton on 1 November 1865, to Sampford Courtenay on 8 January 1871, to Okehampton on 3 October 1871 and to Lydford on 12 October 1874.

Below:
A general view of the LSWR terminus at Plymouth Friary, from Tothill Street bridge, in 1933. The skyline is of the old Plymouth, dominated by the parish church (which escaped destruction). The ground slopes from Beaumont Park on the right to Sutton Harbour, just out of sight on the left. A London express, hauled by a 'T9' class engine, is preparing to start, and a man is on the roof of the dining car filling its tank. Fitters and cleaners are working on coaches in the middle siding. On the right is an 'O2' class engine with one coach on the Turnchapel service. *L&G*

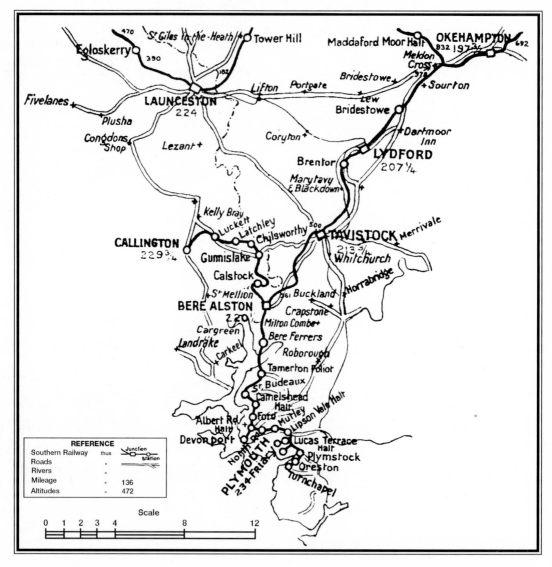

Because of the need to cross the area of high ground which runs northwest from Dartmoor, the route had to ascend all the way with a ruling gradient of 1 in 77, passing high above the town of Okehampton, to reach a summit 950ft above sea level on Sourton Down. There was a length of three miles past the town of North Tawton which was straight; but far from level, as it included a dip over the River Taw and a summit on Halse Moor, both with gradients of 1 in 80 on each side. Further west the builders had to find a way through the hills deeply furrowed by the streams that ran off the heights of Dartmoor,

without exceeding their ruling gradient. They succeeded so well that trains were able to run downhill at high speed — up to 90mph — to compensate in some measure for the long hard pull up. This was achieved at the cost of convenience to the local inhabitants, for the stations of Bow, North Tawton and Sampford Courtenay were all over a mile from the places they purported to serve, and Okehampton station was perched on the windswept slope of Dartmoor, over 200ft above the town.

Near the hamlet of Meldon the line crossed the ravine of the West Okement River by means of a

Right:
The interior of Plymouth Friary at a quiet moment in the year 1913. The stabled rake of coaches, in LSWR brown and salmon livery, bears the set number 197. On the far end is a newer elliptical-roof coach of the type introduced by Surrey Warner. The round marks on the footbridge are flaws on the film. *L&G*

Centre right:
A forecourt view of the main building of Plymouth Friary in 1913. *L&G*

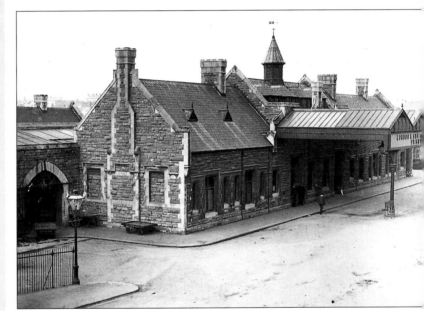

Below right:
A London express at Plymouth North Road, hauled by a somewhat unusual engine. 'L12' class 4-4-0 No 433 was built at Nine Elms in March 1905 and scrapped in November 1951. This shows her original Drummond boiler with firebox water tubes, the ends of which are covered by the square casing. The 'L12' was a 'T9' with a larger boiler, also used in the 'S11' class, and was intended to work on the easier gradients at the eastern end of the South Western. This engine spent the interwar years on the South Eastern, and finished up pottering around Guildford. *LPC*

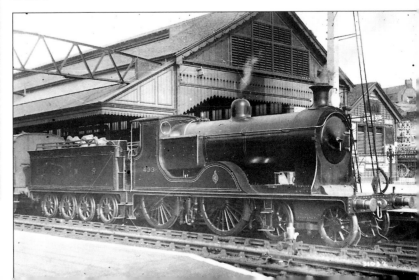

wrought-iron viaduct, 173yd long, of six spans, 113ft above the river. This graceful structure complements a scene of serene beauty, with farmland on one side, the moor rising on the other and the wooded valley beneath. From this airy setting the descent was equally steep to Lydford, where, true to form, the station was well over a mile from the town. It was actually at the south end of Lydford Gorge, a spectacular wooded defile which was, and is, a 'must' for tourists.

Down in Plymouth, the LSWR built a terminal station at Devonport (King's Road) on a short branch off the GWR main line, and a goods station at Friary Gardens near Sutton Pool. Under an agreement between the two companies, the GWR built a curve across the lines converging on its Millbay terminus and laid mixed-gauge track through to Marsh Mills Junction and up to Lydford. South Western trains began running to Devonport on 18 May 1876. Plymouth's station, in the suburb of Mutley, became inadequate for the rise in business, so the GWR built a new station, North Road, most of the cost of which was met by the LSWR. The single line from Coleford Junction to Lydford also proved to be inadequate for its new status, and was doubled over the next three years. This work included building a second viaduct at Meldon, close beside and joined to the original structure. It was made of

steel, but was otherwise similar, and close inspection is necessary to detect the difference.

In 1883 the Plymouth, Devonport & South Western Junction Railway was incorporated to build an independent standard-gauge line from Lydford to Plymouth. The 22-mile line was very expensive owing to the engineering works required: three tunnels, much cutting and banking, 76 bridges and seven viaducts including the 493yd-long Tavy Bridge. The inspector for the Board of Trade, not normally given to enthusiasm, reported that the line was 'more than ordinarily well finished' and 'many of the viaducts and bridges are remarkably handsome'.

The route lay parallel to the existing line down the River Burn to Tavistock, whence it took to the peninsula between the rivers Tamar and Tavy, an area which today remains uniquely isolated and undeveloped. By a brilliant feat of surveying the route kept to a ruling gradient of 1 in 73 down to the Tavy Bridge, by way of a series of great curves including a half-circle round the town of Bere Alston. This also entailed leaving Tavistock folk in the same situation as Okehampton, with a long walk up from the town to the station, and the added bonus of being able to see the trains above them on a massive viaduct. Then it passed through the western suburbs of Plymouth, to emerge from a tunnel under

Right:
'T9' No 733, standing on Plymouth Friary shed in 1932, looks a trifle work-stained. Because the 'T9s' were very useful engines they were worked hard and sometimes ended up, as here, with the paint burnt off the smokebox door by hot cinders piling up inside. The impressive wheel visible on the tender front is the handbrake. The small letter 'H' behind the buffer beam is a power-rating code. *LGRP/NRM*

Centre right:
No 733 in much better external condition, together with another 'T9', hauling a Barnstaple-Exeter train at Yeoford in 1937. *LGRP/NRM*

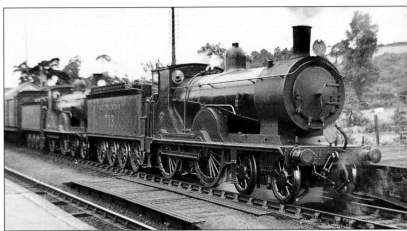

Below right:
The quay sidings around Plymouth were worked by the small but powerful 'B4' class 0-4-0Ts. They were fitted with wire basket spark arrestors in the top of the chimney, as seen on No 84, standing outside Friary engine shed in 1949. This is one of the later members of the class, and was moreover the last engine built at Nine Elms Works, in June 1908. She was based at Plymouth throughout her career. *L&G*

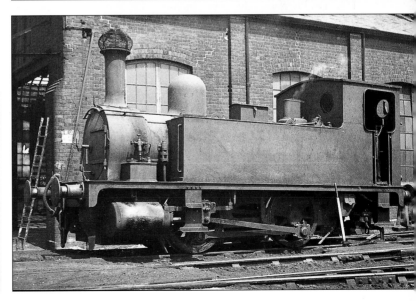

Above:
The Turnchapel branch was worked by 'Gate' stock, so called because of their entrance vestibules with low wrought-iron doors. One such, No 369, is standing at Lucas Terrace Halt on 22 May 1935. Its position with only the tail end by the platform and the guard's door open suggests that it might have been drawn up for the photographer. The engine is 'O2' class 0-4-4T No 207, fitted with air control apparatus for push-pull working. The steps lead up to the halt from Lucas Terrace. Behind the shelter is Friary engine shed, and a 'T9' class engine is being turned on the turntable. *H. C. Casserley*

Right:
A freight working from Turnchapel carrying timbers. The special sleeper wagon is amply provided with chains, whereas those in the open wagon behind are stacked over one end and roped down. The engine is 'B4' No 88, one of the earlier batch built at Nine Elms in 1892. The date is 9 April 1956; the location is near Oreston. *P. F. Bowles*

Devonport Park into what had been the back end of King's Road station. This lower end tangled with the Cornwall Railway line like a piece of metallic knitting: under the Royal Albert Bridge, under again at Trelawney Place, looping round Weston Mill Lake, and under again, this time in a tunnel. At St Budeaux station the tracks were only 10yd apart, but there was no connection until a crossover was laid at the beginning of 1941. Similarly, at the top end the new line lay alongside the

Launceston & South Devon from Lydford for over five miles to Harford Bridge, giving the appearance of a three-track line; but the only connection was by a short shunting neck in Lydford station.

The line was leased to the London & South Western, and when its trains were switched to this route on 2 June 1890 they reversed direction through Plymouth. In the following year Friary station was improved for passenger use and a curve was provided for trains to run

into it from Devonport. (In the interim they had to terminate at Mutley.)

As it passed under the bridge at North Road station a down South Western train was heading northeast, having completed seven-eighths of a full circle since leaving Exeter, and it traversed another half-circle to reach its destination. If you saw a goods train going through North Road you could walk across the town in time to see it arrive at Friary.

Devonport and Friary stations had a common feature: from the middle of the goods sidings a branch descended into a tunnel under the yard forecourt to gain access to the waterfront. The branch from Devonport served quays down the west bank of Stonehouse Pool, and that from Friary went to Sutton Harbour. One of the contents of the complex agreement between the two companies was a division of any custom they could tempt off passing transatlantic ships: the GWR got the mails and the LSWR got the passengers. Those who were

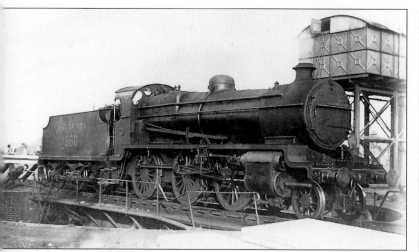

Left:
At Friary shed on 5 July 1926, two men (one out of sight at the near end) turning one of the new 'N' class on the hand-operated turntable. No A860 was one of the Woolwich Arsenal engines assembled in 1925. *EWJC*

Below left:
Devonport King's Road station was an imposing structure with a massive overall roof. This view, taken in 1907, is from King's Road, showing the western end with the PDSWJ line coming into it from the tunnel. *L&G*

Below:
The station built for the LSWR by the GWR on its own main line: Plymouth North Road. This view from the east end was in 1921, during one of the enlargements which gradually filled the site and eliminated such peripheral activities as growing vegetables. The coaches are indeed Great Western, for this was in the period when the famous brown and cream livery was replaced by all-over brown. *LGRP/NRM*

Right:
Bridestowe station was close by the slopes of Dartmoor. This view northeast in the up direction looks towards Southerly Down. The main building (from the near end: office, booking hall, ladies' waiting room and lavatory with stationmaster's house behind and over, and gentlemen's lavatory) was a standard design which appeared on all the lines west of Exeter. At this time, 1949, the station had received a footbridge of the concrete type prefabricated at Exmouth Junction, which was probably viewed as a modernistic eyesore when it appeared. *L&G*

in a tearing hurry to reach London from America were brought in to Stonehouse by tenders. There they boarded a special train which was hauled up to Devonport by a shunting engine and then rushed to Waterloo. A station was built for these VIPs at Stonehouse and to celebrate its opening the 'Ocean Liner' special of 23 April 1904 ran from Devonport to Waterloo in 4hr 3min.

With a route from London to Plymouth 16 miles shorter than that of the rival GWR, the LSWR looked set fair for new prosperity, and indeed its principal expresses, the 11am from Waterloo (5hr 45min to Plymouth) and the 10.15am from Plymouth (6hr 55min to Waterloo), were faster than the GWR service. But it was handicapped by having to reach a high point on the slopes of Dartmoor, at 950ft above sea level. The ascent from the Tavy Bridge to Bere Alston, four miles at 1 in 73, was more severe than the more famous Shap Incline in the north of England, and was followed by a further 19 miles of climbing. The only consolation was that it was less steep than the Great Western's 1 in 42 from Plympton to Hemerdon. Another disadvantage was that owing to the limited budget of the builders there were weight restrictions, principally on Meldon Viaduct, which prevented the employment of bigger engines after the

Drummond 'S11' class of 1903. As train weights increased and the GWR improved its route to London, the LSWR fell behind in capturing goods and passengers from Plymouth — the only really lucrative traffic in the West Country. Not until 1945 was the gap closed with a locomotive, the Bulleid 'West Country' class, that could haul a heavy, fast train right through from Plymouth to London. While North Road station and the GWR freight facilities at Millbay and Tavistock Junction were enlarged during the 1930s, Friary retained its air of a quiet backwater. Eventually the Plymouth portions of South Western trains were no more important than those for North Devon and North Cornwall.

The mountainous nature of the line precipitated two accidents which could have been far more disastrous than they were. On the evening of 30 March 1875 a train was climbing towards Sampford Moors from the viaduct over the River Taw when the engine coupling broke. The coaches at once ran back down the hill, this being before the introduction of automatic brakes. The guard took no action, claiming subsequently that he thought that the driver was merely backing to take a run at the bank, and the coaches ran through the dip and up the other side to North Tawton. By good luck they halted before reaching the summit, beyond

which nothing would have stopped them, and ran forward again. Meanwhile the driver, realising he had lost his train, continued until he decided it could not be following him, then set out very cautiously backwards. He had passed the viaduct when the coaches appeared and crashed into the engine. Happily, only three people were injured. On 6 March 1898 an Exeter-Plymouth express was running fast downhill towards Tavistock when the engine, 'M7' class 0-4-4T No 252, came off the track and took the whole train with her, luckily without serious casualties. The same thing had happened three years before with an engine of similar type on the Great Western; the practice of using tank engines to haul express trains, hitherto common, was disapproved because of this accident and many companies ceased to do so.

In the area around the Tamar Valley were numerous interests, particularly farming and mining, anxious to improve their rail connections. They persuaded Parliament to

Above:
A down train, hauled by a 'T9', entering Bridestowe early in the century. The photographer is clearly a rarer sight than the train. In the distance a goods is shunting on the up line. To the right of its steam is a gate giving access to the Rattlebrook Peat Railway, a horse-worked line which climbed onto the top of Dartmoor. (Issued as a postcard by Chapman & Son, Dawlish.) *EWJC*

Above right:
A view of Meldon Viaduct dating from about 1910, showing a down train hauled by an Adams 4-4-0. At that time the West Okement valley was a mess of ruined kilns, roadways, excavations, spoil tips, and detritus of many ages of mineral working. *EWJC*

include in the PDSWJ Act a requirement to purchase, one year after its own main line was opened, the East Cornwall Mineral Railway. This ran from Calstock Quay to Kelly Bray, north of Callington. It was to have been a broad gauge line, on which work started in the year

46

1863, but the company collapsed, was reformed in 1869 and completed the line as a 3ft 6in gauge railway. It opened on 8 May 1872. The terminus was originally intended to be at Callington, but it was never built, so the Kelly Bray terminus was named Callington instead. The principal traffic was the arsenic, copper, lead, tin and wolfram from the mines of Kit Hill and the line made a half-circle round the 1,094ft summit. A 700yd-long 1 in 6 incline was needed to descend from Drakewalls, over 400ft above sea level, to the Tamar at Calstock.

Various plans to connect the ECMR to the rest of the railway system came to nothing, and the company was wound up when, in 1891, the PDSWJ purchase came into effect. The new owners devised a scheme to take advantage of the creation of the Light Railway Commission in 1896; a Bere Alston & Calstock Light Railway Order was obtained for a line from the main line at Bere Alston to the existing route near Drakewalls. To oversee the project the company

appointed the man who had made the light railway business particularly his own, Colonel Holman F. Stephens. The work proceeded very slowly, however, and was not completed until early in 1908. In the middle of it they decided to change to standard gauge and the ECMR was converted so that the reopening train on 12 March 1908 ran through from Bere Alston to Callington.

The new section was in plan an almost perfect S-shape with some extra curves thrown in, taking over four miles to join points two miles apart. It included the famous viaduct at Calstock, with twelve 60ft spans carrying the rails 120ft above the river. It was made of concrete blocks, a novel material at the time, and was widely held to have spoilt the scenery of the Tamar Valley, already popular with tourists. Passengers on the line had ample time to enjoy the view, as the curves and gradients of 1 in 39 on the Bere Alston side and 1 in 38 on the Calstock side imposed caution on the trains. The incline was abandoned and to provide access to

47

Left:
At Meldon Quarry the Civil Engineer's Department had a shunting engine, stabled in a small shed. This shows 'O2' 0-4-4T No 232 from Exmouth Junction at home on 6 July 1948, standing in for the resident shunter, which was London, Chatham & Dover Railway 'T' class 0-6-0T No 1607. The shed looks ramshackle even for that class of building; not long after, it was replaced by a concrete structure just as ugly but more solid. *J. H. Aston*

Centre left:
In June 1950 the 52-year-old 'G6' class No 272, recently overhauled, was allocated to Meldon Quarry as No DS3152, and served there for 10 years. *G. Wheeler*

Below left:
No 272 at work in Meldon Quarry on 4 June 1959, in the middle of what looks like a rather curious movement. She is propelling the 4.15pm stone train out of the yard. The coach is provided for taking staff home to Okehampton. 'T9' No 30726 appears hardly adequate for such a massive load, but only has to brake it down to Okehampton. *J. H. Aston*

Right:
The Civil Engineers in possession near Brentor in July 1927. Their staff transport is made up of old oil-lit coaches. One may deduce from the scene, with the foreman (in bowler hat) walking towards the train, that they are finishing their task; in which case the crane driver will be lowering his jib onto the match-truck.
EWJC

the quay a wagon lift was erected alongside the viaduct. However, after the first few years it was seldom used, so it was dismantled in 1934, by which time commercial traffic on the river was a past memory.

Although the PDSWJ company handed the operating of its main line to the LSWR from the outset, it worked the Callington branch itself. At first it retained Colonel Stephens as Manager, but as that peripatetic gentleman did not give it the attention desired, his connection was severed in 1910. The company was absorbed into the new Southern Railway in 1923.

The ECMR had two engines, built by Neilson & Co in 1871; one was sold for scrap after the conversion, but the other was converted to standard gauge by the railway staff at Callington. In this form she was not a success, and was sold in 1912 to Colonel Stephens. For its reincarnation as a standard gauge line the company bought some second-hand four-wheeled coaches from the LSWR and three new engines from Hawthorn, Leslie & Co. One, a 0-6-0T, was numbered 3 and named *A. S. Harris*, and worked on the line until 1929, when she was superseded by engines of the LSWR 'O2' class. Nos 4 *Earl of Mount Edgcumbe* and 5 *Lord St Levan* (these names were directors of the company) were 0-6-2T engines. They were very powerful for their size and worked the line capably until 1957.

The stations were provided with modest corrugated-iron buildings in the Stephens style, but Callington boasted a smart timber roof intended to house the passenger train overnight, and an engine shed. Gunnislake, as the station at Drakewalls was called, was unusual in having an island platform entered via a subway. Calstock was tucked in at the north end of the viaduct. Other stations were at Chilsworthy, Cox Park (named Latchley) and Monk's Cross (named Luckett).

Over the years the line continued in much the same way, with five to seven passenger and two goods trains each day. With its tremendous curves, gradients and spectacular views it was the most impressive of the West Country branches, and the journey had an air of adventure as it climbed out of the Tamar Valley. It would have been a splendid attraction if operated by a preservation society, in which role the remote site of its terminus, so unsatisfactory commercially, would have been a positive advantage.

Remote outpost as it was, Plymouth Friary was not the end of the line. Just short of the terminus a branch line turned south down the Cattewater, crossed it at Laira Bridge and described yet another half-circle to Turnchapel. The approach to the terminus, a swing bridge over the mouth of Hooe Lake, had the distinction of being the most southerly point on the Southern Railway.

Right:

Shunting goods wagons at Okehampton with an Adams '395' class 'Express Goods'. This one was No 69, built in 1885 by Nielson & Co of Glasgow. She was renumbered 83 in 1889 and 083 in 1908. The significance of the '0' is that the engine had been written off the company's capital stock, although she continued to work for another 45 years. In 1929 she was rebuilt with a boiler recovered from a scrapped South Eastern Railway engine, and is shown in that form. The roof on the Okehampton footbridge was a desirable feature, as from that position there was nothing much between you and the USA. *RPC*

Centre right:

Tavistock on a wet Devon day, 5 June 1959. 'T9' class No 30702 pulls away past the goods yard and heads for the moors with the Plymouth portion of the 'Atlantic Coast Express'. *J. H. Aston*

Below right:

Bere Alston station in Southern days. Such is the curvature of the route that at this point the camera is looking due east towards Mount Tamar. As usual for these photographs, the staff are on parade, grouped round a barrow loaded with boxes of strawberries. There is an intriguing poster on the end wall of the up platform waiting room, depicting a 78rpm shellac gramophone record surmounting the outline of Southern England. Note the spelling — 'Bear'. In the 19th century it was 'Beer'. (Issued as a postcard by Chapman & Son, Dawlish.) *EWJC*

Left:
At Bere Alston in 1937: a local train from Plymouth has delivered its passengers and the engine is about to remove it. 'O2' class 0-4-4T No 232 was one of the last built, in 1895, and was usually found working around Exeter. The station footbridge is an ungainly combination of standard concrete stair sections with a South Western lattice span. *LGRP/NRM*

Below left:
The two PDSWJ Hawthorn Leslie 0-6-2Ts outside their shed at Callington. It is likely that they have been positioned for the photograph, for *Earl of Mount Edgcumbe* in the foreground is blocking the exit for *Lord St Levan*. Someone is shovelling coal from the wagon behind her. *LPC*

Above right:
Callington terminus in 1950. The engine shed is in the foreground and the near object is a water column. Beyond is the passenger station, with the original platform extended beyond the roof by the Southern. *L&G*

Centre right:
East Cornwall Mineral Railway No 2, built by Neilson in 1877; one of the two engines operated on the original 3ft 6in gauge track. *L&G*

Below right:
The same engine rebuilt to run on the standard gauge. Even assuming that they bought such items as wheelsets or even complete frame plates, the conversion was a remarkable feat to carry out at Callington shed. *LPC*

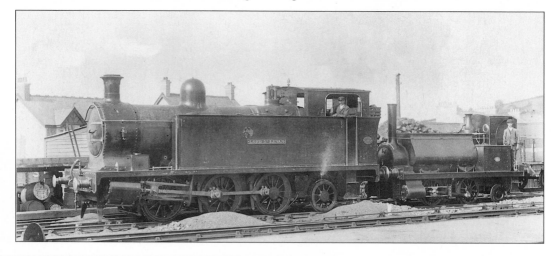

Above:
Proof that No 2 did indeed run on standard gauge rails is this view of her with one of the replacements, *Lord St Levan*. Perhaps the placing of a young fireman on board is by way of a hint that she is not man enough for the job. LPC/NRM

Centre left:
In the British railway mind there has always been a distinction, in every operating aspect, between goods and passengers, so the mixed train has never been favoured. A rarity was this adaptation by the PDSWJR from a six-wheeled coach, combining goods brake van equipment with seating. In this view it is running as SR No 54962. *LGRP/NRM*

Left:
Just after the Bere Alston link was opened in 1908, the Hawthorn Leslie engine *A. S. Harris* hauls the ex-LSWR coaches across Calstock Viaduct, with everything bright and new. The winch of the wagon hoist appears on the right; a ship lying at the quay is glimpsed through the arches. *LGRP/NRM*

Above:
The Calstock Incline soon became a piece of industrial archaeology. This bridge over a lane near the bottom of the incline was photographed in 1950.
L&G

Above right:
After operations ceased on 1 March 1908 the incline top station, just off the Calstock-Norris Green road, was left in peace. The buildings are seen in 1950. On the left is the engine shed, in the right background the incline winding house. The track passed round the high water tower to the incline top immediately behind it.
L&G

Centre right:
A close-up of Hawthorn Leslie *Earl of Mount Edgcumbe* in Southern days, on Plymouth Friary shed in 1932. Products of a firm which built for industry, these engines were robust and easily serviced.
LGRP/NRM

Below right:
The ECMR station at Latchley survived the rebuilding, when a new station was provided off to the right, and indeed survived the railway to become a private house.
LGRP/NRM

Left:
The little halt at Chilsworthy was one of those places that saw no appreciable change from beginning to end. This was taken in July 1964, two years before closure, when it had acquired an enamel nameboard, concrete fence posts to hold the lamps and a BR 'whistle' and 10mph sign. *A. Muckley*

Below:
At Bere Alston station on 7 April 1953, passengers and staff wait for 'O2' class No 30236 to shunt the Callington branch train from the siding to the back platform, for the 10.50am departure. The steam drifting across is either from the up 'Atlantic Coast Express', which called at 10.23, or from the 8.41am Exeter-Plymouth stopping train, which called at 10.37. *R. E. Vincent*

4. North Cornwall

It took 35 years to get railway tracks out to the North Cornish coast; 35 years later the network was at its height as part of the Southern's grand plan to give every Londoner a chance to enjoy the country, and vice versa; 35 years after that it was discarded and forgotten.

When the Devon & Cornwall Railway had completed its main line to Lydford, the contractor, Relf, started work in August 1875 on another route for which the company had statutory powers, a branch to Holsworthy. Extensions to Bodmin, Bude, etc, were also authorised but were beyond the financial reach of impoverished Cornwall. Even the Holsworthy section could not have been built if landowners had not donated the land for it, so convinced were they of the prosperity it would bring to their estates. The line was opened on 20 January 1879.

The North Cornwall Railway Co, formed in late 1882, was a local venture supported by the wealthy families: the Molesworths of Wadebridge, the Prideaux-Brunes of Padstow, the Gurneys of Bude, and many more. The engineering firm which designed and built it, Galbraith & Church, was also retained by the LSWR, and it was accepted from the start that the latter would work the line. However, the company stayed constitutionally independent until the 1923 Grouping.

This was no small undertaking; from Halwill, on the Holsworthy branch, to Padstow was 50 miles, as far as London to Brighton. The railway was built in four stages, each set up under separate statutory powers and legally a separate entity. They were:

1. Halwill to Launceston, opened on 20 July 1886;
2. Launceston to Delabole, commenced in 1890 and itself opened in stages to Tresmeer on 28 July 1892, to Camelford on 14 August 1893 and to Delabole on 18 October 1893;
3. Delabole to Wadebridge, commenced in late 1893 and opened on 31 May 1895, although the ceremonial opening was on 12 June;
4. Wadebridge to Padstow, commenced in 1896 and opened on 23 March 1899.

There was reason in this progression. Launceston, market and administrative centre for East Cornwall, had already acquired a taste for modern communications with the arrival of a line from Tavistock in 1865. Delabole Quarry and other slate and stone workings around it formed the only source of heavy mineral traffic and one which could make good use of rail transport. The quarry owners invested heavily in the NCR. Wadebridge, owned by the South Western on paper, was falling under the spell of

Below:
The first terminus of the drive to Cornwall was Holsworthy, which of course is still in Devon. The tracks came to an end just beyond the signal, on the brink of a deep valley. The extension involved a sharp right turn and descent to Derriton Viaduct. Cattle wagons, seen in the yard, were always here serving the principal market of the area. This view was taken in 1931. *L&G*

the Great Western. Padstow was an ancient port, the safest haven on a coastline which exacted a steady toll in vessels and lives (and still does). The illogical aspect, as it appears from the map, is why the company built the Halwill-Launceston section instead of making use of the lines which already existed via Lydford. The answer is that it tried to, but the South Devon Railway would not agree to it. In due course the company was to pay dearly for this political diversion. It is sad but true that, no matter how much lip service is paid to the preservation of the environment, when they make a journey people will do their utmost to take the most direct and fastest route. The train journey from Launceston to Okehampton was 26 miles (with a wait while the Bude portion was attached) against 19 by road, and that was the sort of handicap road hauliers were later encouraged to exploit.

Bude did eventually get its railway; an extension from Holsworthy was opened on 10 August 1898. The long interlude left a legacy of technological contrast in Holsworthy. The station was sited actually in the town, which stood above a confluence of two streams. The route crossed both and thus required a viaduct on each side. The eastern one, built in 1878, was of stone and brick construction, but the western one, built 20 years later, was made of concrete blocks. This and the similar viaduct at Woolston were the first large-scale structures using this material, and set an excellent example of utilitarian but graceful style. It was copied shortly afterwards at Calstock, but already engineers were developing the technique of using mass concrete, so this trio are the only specimens of their type.

A ruling gradient of 1 in 78 was adopted in the initial surveys, but for the Bude extension

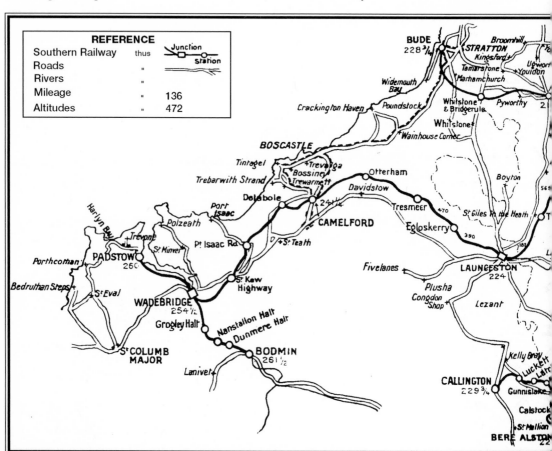

and the North Cornwall it was amended to 1 in 73 — and plenty of it. From Meldon down to sea level at Bude in 29 miles means an average gradient of 1 in 160. That may not seem much to readers whose only experience of vehicles is in motor-cars, but it would be ample to send a train, in the absence of any restraint, out into the mouth of the River Neet. The station was placed in the meadows beside the Stratton road. As usual, the townspeople objected to the railway coming into the centre and afterwards complained that it was too far away. However, only goods wagons went any farther. One of the objects of the promoters was to usurp the position of the Bude Canal, which had proved disappointing from the profit angle and was already derelict 70 years after opening. They constructed a short branch across to the canal basin, for direct loading from ships and also from a 4ft gauge tramway which brought sea

sand up from the beach. None of the holidaymakers who now jam their cars into the site of the siding realises that until World War 2 coastal shipping was an everyday and important means of transport.

Except for Holsworthy, whose station was as convenient as could be wished, there were no towns of any size in the area. The position of Halwill Junction was determined by the lie of the land, which permitted a descent at the ruling gradient into the valley of the River Carey to reach Launceston. Approaching the town, the train crossed over the South Devon branch, by now part of the GWR. Although the latter led to Plymouth, it was a branch line with a branch line service, and of course the journey via Halwill and Okehampton was impossibly circuitous. This failure to connect Launceston to the commercial centre of the whole Southwest, only 25 miles away, was responsible for the

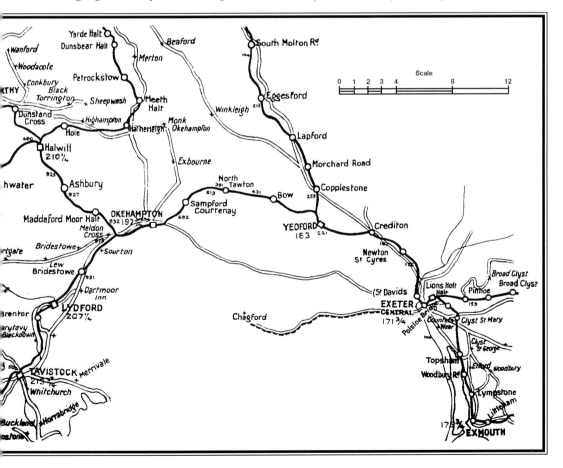

decline of the town before the introduction of the motor-car and the decline of the railway after.

From the low-level crossing of the River Tamar at Polson, the NCR climbed to a summit 860ft above sea level at Trewanion. It descended the Allen Valley to Egloshayle, where it joined the original route of the Bodmin & Wadebridge. Wadebridge station was enlarged, provided with an extra platform and a new engine shed on ground reclaimed from the riverside meadow.

At Padstow a level site was obtained on the foreshore just above the harbour by cutting back the bank and filling on the waterside. In 1902 the LSWR built a large shed for the fish market on this ground, and a new quay alongside was completed in 1912. It then built a new jetty, 800ft long and 40ft wide, out into the water parallel with the quay. The Southern Railway continued to improve the quays through the 1920s and 1930s, and as late as 1947 built a protuberance into the estuary to accommodate a new turntable for the 'West Country' class engines. Above the station rose a huge hotel as grand as any in Torquay — the South Western — financed by another wealthy Padstow family, the Corys. It opened in the

Above:
Holsworthy Viaduct from the south on 25 July 1957. The 1.18pm Okehampton-Bude is formed of a two-coach set, an extra corridor third coach and a four-wheel parcels van, hauled by 'T9' No 30717. This train connected with the mid-morning Plymouth-Exeter and Exeter-Plymouth services. *S. C. Nash*

Above right:
Halwill for Beaworthy, the proper name of what most folk call Halwill Junction, lay in the middle of sparsely populated countryside and saw few train services for much of the year. However, there was usually something going on, and even the horse appears interested in the operations in this 1931 view. A Bude train has arrived and the engine has run round and is coupling to the other end. *L&G*

summer of 1901. Possibly the railway objected to the implied connection in the title, as it was renamed the Metropole in 1908.

An oddity of the line was that the more important stations were the less impressive. At Okehampton, Halwill, Launceston and Wadebridge a single-storey office building was provided. Elsewhere the stationmaster lived 'over the shop' and business was done in an annexe to what was, in total, a bigger building. The design of the house was found all over the

Right:
Camelford station lay in the open country characteristic of the North Cornish coast, some 750ft above sea level. It was the station for the romantic shrine of Tintagel, a privilege which merited a platform canopy, though not a footbridge. To the right are the stone goods shed and Olde's store, with railway staff houses beyond. This view, taken in 1931, is looking inland towards Davidstowe Moor. *L&G*

Right:
The standard station house at Port Isaac Road. There were 10 on the NCR, three like this and the others built as mirror images. In this 1950 view it shows little sign of the passage of years. *LGRP/NRM*

South Western and very handsome it was. It and the staff houses erected at every station by the company were conspicuously superior to the average dwelling.

When looking at the way the line wound through the hills, it is essential, for those brought up in an age when a few men with diesel-engined machinery can remove a hill without breaking sweat, to understand what a tremendous achievement it was. Cornish rock

is tough stuff. The engineers had to strike a balance between the cost of digging through it and the future benefits of a straight road. To bring a large number of men to the site, to house and feed them, to shift excavated rock from cutting to embankment and to move building materials on an unprecedented scale was a massive problem in what is now called logistics. Of course, in those days the word 'environment' was unknown; the railway

Left:
The public entrance to the standard building, seen from the forecourt at Padstow.
LGRP/NRM

Below:
Halwill, Ashbury and Dunsland Cross were more meagrely equipped. This shows Dunsland Cross in 1931, just after the loop had been extended beyond the platforms; it was a bleak place in an area of high ground and took the full impact of winter weather.
LGRP/NRM

Right:
In 1925 the Southern Railway embarked on a publicity programme, which included naming its largest express engines, the 'N15' class, after people and places from the King Arthur legend. This is No 745 *Tintagel*, built at Eastleigh in 1919, as running after 1927 with Southern chimney and exhaust-lifting plates. She never went nearer Tintagel than Exeter, 55 miles away. *LPC*

Above:
The wide-open feel of the countryside on the North Cornish coast is captured in this view at Port Isaac Road on 31 May 1960. The arriving train is the 1.15am from Waterloo; 'N' class No 31840 hauling a two-coach local set, followed by the through coach and newspaper van. *J. H. Aston*

Left:
A prospective passenger's view of the new Wadebridge station, built by the LSWR in 1888 when the line from Bodmin was improved. To its right is the goods shed. To its left is the platform, added in 1895 when the NCR arrived, and the wooden engine shed. *LGRP/NRM*

Centre left:
Wadebridge station in its final form was quite large. This 1948 view of the east end shows the full range of facilities: cattle pen, goods shed, three platforms, water tower, two-road engine shed. The impressive bracket signal controls the exits from the two up platforms to two single lines which run parallel to Wadebridge Junction. *L&G*

Below:
In the summer of 1913, Padstow was on the way to prosperity and the railway was expanding. Space was left between the station and the fish shed, and an extra siding had already been laid in it. A London express, hauled by an Adams 4-4-0, is starting away, with the cylinder drain cocks open to clear out condensed water. *LGRP/NRM*

builders thought no more of the impact of their work than did the miners of the appearance of their diggings and tailings, and no doubt if they had been given the means to carve a road several hundred feet wide through the heart of Bodmin Moor they would have done it.

Just occasionally the hills were responsible for spectacular events. In February 1905 a freight train became divided while running from Meldon to Halwill. By the time the crew discovered this, the front part had drawn some way ahead; but the back part then accelerated down the gradient and crashed into the front, resulting in a massive pile of smashed wagons just south of Halwill station. In December 1893 a rake of 23 wagons carrying cattle, parked on the NCR line outside Halwill during shunting manoeuvres, ran away down the Carey Valley but luckily stopped on an up-grade approaching Tower Hill. The escape record was held by six wagons and a brake van which got away from Otterham and ran down through Tresmeer, Egloskerry and Launceston and fetched up at Tower Hill 17 miles away. They finally came to rest in the bottom at Polson Bridge. On the wet night of 19 November 1898 the driver of 'Jubilee' class 0-4-2 No 535, coming down to Tresmeer with a freight, found he could not stop, and was pushed on until meeting head-on the evening passenger train; happily, again without serious casualties. All these accidents happened in winter. The weather in that country is not to be underrated at any time, certainly not when winter storms sweep in from the Atlantic and flay the exposed uplands.

Right:
A view westwards on Wadebridge station in 1913. The original B&W terminus lay in the distance between the platforms and the high buildings which are in Molesworth Street; its buildings survive, on the left of the track. In front of them stands a steam rail motor of Class H13, probably No 4 or 5, taking water. One of these was run on Bodmin-Padstow services from 1908 until 1919. *L&G*

Beow right:
Padstow station in 1950, deserted except for a solitary staff member whose mind appears to be on gardening. A detail is that the bedroom window is open, showing that the arch in the stonework is ornamental and the wooden sash window frame is shaped to match. In the background, overlooking the harbour, is the Metropole Hotel. *L&G*

Left:
Padstow's charming signalbox, a stone version of the LSWR standard design. *T. M. Walsh*

Below:
A view of Padstow taken about 1950. The small goods yard is off to the left. 'T9' No 30712, built by Dubs in 1899, hauls 1935 coaches Nos 2790 and 6691, now running as a two-coach set; another set is in the siding with seven other coaches. Behind them is the fish shed, and visible over its roof are some of the buildings round the harbour. On the right, still looking fresh and new, is the 1947 turntable. The tide is high in the Camel estuary. Above the left-hand edge of the water tank is Padstow's War Memorial. *B. A. Butt*

Right:
The LSWR built 17 steam railcars for use on branch lines, and this is No 10 on trial at Padstow when new in 1906. The small engine with 10in cylinders mounted on one bogie can be seen. The boiler was behind the louvres. The railcars were never satisfactory; they suffered from lack of power and bad riding, and were difficult to service and keep clean, and were given up after about 10 years. The Bodmin-Padstow service was the last to use them, from which they were withdrawn in May 1918. *LGRP/NRM*

Centre right:
Beattie tank No 30586 runs alongside the Camel estuary on 2 July 1954, approaching Wadebridge with the Saturday 11.55am from Padstow. The coaches are Nos 2792 and 6575; the latter was the first coach to arrive on the Bluebell Railway in 1960 for the commencement of services by the Preservation Society. The 5½-mile run on the level was within the capability of the little engine, but something bigger would be put on to take the train on to Okehampton. *S. C. Nash*

Below right:
Bude had a more elaborate station house than most on the 'Withered Arm', resembling those of (for example) Sidmouth or Swanage. The line-up of a carter and two local cabs is clearly designed to impress potential visitors, although the elegance is marred by the corrugated-iron hut which is the shunter's cabin. On the left the line of white posts marks where the quay branch runs down to the canal basin. The building on the far side of the meadows is the lifeboat station. *IAL*

Above:
On Bude platform in 1923. The dramatic gesture by the shunter is probably for the driver of an engine approaching behind us in the course of running round the coaches. There appears to be an imbalance in the working of teacups, as they have filled a basket with them for return up the line. *L&G*

Below:
Shunting Bude Quay on 7 September 1956, using a new British Railways 2-6-2T No 82011; propelling very carefully across the road by the canal bridge. *M. R. Galley*

Above:
From 1925 the principal all-purpose locomotive on the Bude and North Cornwall lines was the 'N' class. In June 1949 No 31833 pulls out of Halwill with a seven-coach train from Padstow and Bude. The loop in the foreground gave access to the wartime storage sidings. This engine had an encounter with this loop on 16 June 1944. She was accidentally routed into it, and the driver could not stop before he reached the far end and she fell into the Beaworthy road.
S. C. Nash

Below:
Okehampton locomotive depot was enlarged in 1920 and again in 1947, when a new coal stage and a 70ft powered turntable were installed. On 19 July 1949 a fireman is coupling his engine's vacuum pipe to the turntable motor. 'U' class 2-6-0 No 31628 was built at Ashford in 1929, one of the many engines incorporating parts made by Woolwich Arsenal after World War 1. *J. H. Meredith*

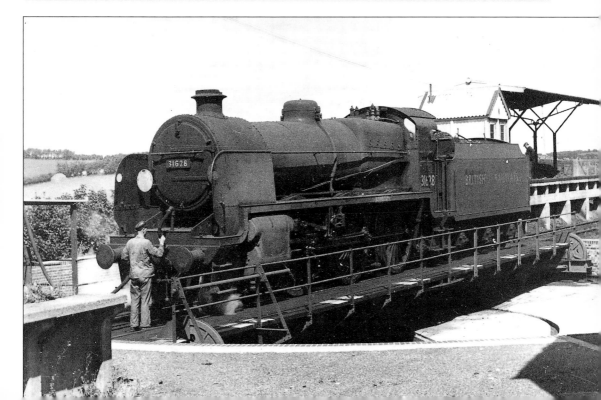

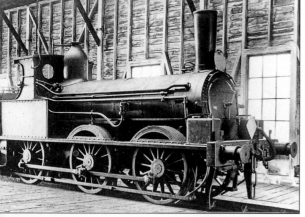

Above:
Barnstaple Junction in 1913, with the original line to Fremington and the Ilfracombe line curving round to the right. The lack of space made for a far from satisfactory layout. The station had two platforms with three tracks passing between them; the coach on the left is standing on a short siding. In 1924 the up platform was given another track round the back, and that splendid tower of a signalbox was replaced by a conventional box. *LGRP/NRM*

Centre left:
'Ilfracombe Goods' No 394 in the timber engine shed at Barnstaple in the year 1907. The photograph was taken to mark the withdrawal of the class from working the Ilfracombe line. No 394 was supplied by Beyer, Peacock & Co in December 1880. She was stored out of use in 1913, and sold in 1918 to Colonel Stephens, who put her on the East Kent Railway. *L&G*

Left:
This view of No 394 was probably taken on the East Kent Railway; the lettering looks as if it was painted on to the photograph. The dented boiler cladding, wasted and patched smokebox door and split buffer beam are not what one would expect to see on the South Western. *IAL*

5. Ilfracombe

In the fever of the railway promotions of the 1840s, Ilfracombe, the only decent natural harbour on the south side of the Bristol Channel, was viewed as a potential major port, and was mentioned as the ultimate end of the line from London to Exeter. In the year 1860, with a railway to Barnstaple well established and proving its worth, local people looked into an extension to Ilfracombe and surveyed a route. Nothing came of it, partly because Ilfracombe as a community was not much interested and partly because of implacable opposition by Sir William Williams of Heanton Court, on the north shore of the Taw estuary, who owned enough land on the proposed route to block it. Not until that gentleman died in 1870 could the scheme go ahead, and only then after the Barnstaple & Ilfracombe Railway Co had persuaded the

LSWR to work the line when completed. The latter formally bought up the former before it was opened on 21 July 1874.

Although only 15 miles long, it had some large engineering works. It branched off the west end of Barnstaple station and curved round the back of the goods yard to the River Taw, which it crossed on a long bridge, also curved through nearly 90°. There was no requirement for navigation, so the bridge was as low above the water as possible. It might have made more sense to go straight into the north side of the goods yard, but that would have meant doing something nasty to the 13th-century road bridge and no-one in Barnstaple would have tolerated that. As it was, the station had to be expanded on the down side by digging into the hill. Reaching the north bank of the Taw, they headed downriver. The River Yeo,

Right:
The 'Ilfracombe Goods' were replaced by standard Adams 0-6-0s on goods work; on 5 June 1926 No 0397 enters Barnstaple Junction with a goods train of a nominal sort. Built by Neilson in 1881, No 397 was put in the duplicate list in July 1903, but continued to work for another 50 years. *M. W. Earley*

Left:
'T1' class 0-4-4T No 4, in one of a series of photographs taken at Strawberry Hill in 1921. This engine, built at Nine Elms in June 1894 for London commuter trains, was one of several employed on the Ilfracombe line from 1907 until World War 1, when they were replaced by the more powerful 'M7' class. She then returned to London until transfer to the Somerset & Dorset Railway in World War 2. She was scrapped in 1946. Behind is 'O2' No 221. *LPC*

just below the town, served as a dock, so they had to build a swing bridge across its mouth. The route lay level down to Braunton, where it turned inland through the village and up the narrow valley of the River Caen. It went over the watershed at 600ft without even a summit tunnel, to drop into the Slade Valley. This, virtually a ravine, was at an early date filled with water to supply Ilfracombe, and there was no lack of pressure in the taps. The railway did not reach the harbour; it stopped a mile short of it and 250ft above it. As an example of the British habit of spending a vast sum to provide a transport link to a port and then nullifying the thing by not finishing it off, this was not unusual — think of Brixham — but if rails had been projected onto the quays the potential customers might not have used them anyway — think of Newquay. Be that as it may, freight business was never significant in comparison with passengers. The view from the station was magnificent, if you were in a mood to enjoy it; but if you could not walk up hills you would not have gone to the North Devon coast.

All railway builders were under tremendous pressure at that time to save money rather than look to long-term benefits. The result was a lightly-constructed permanent way with sharp curves and very unfavourable gradient profiles. In order to haul trains over the gradients of 1 in 40 from Braunton and 1 in 36 from Ilfracombe to the summit near Mortehoe station, locomotives were needed which were light,

powerful and with good brakes. The LSWR drew up a specification for a 0-6-0 type and the firm of Beyer, Peacock & Co pointed out that it could meet this with a design it was currently building for export. Eight were purchased between 1873 and 1880 and were known as the 'Ilfracombe Goods'. They met the criteria pretty well, and after they were superseded by more powerful locomotives on the Ilfracombe line, they were bought by the light railway owner Colonel Stephens. Subsequently, standard locomotives of the 'T1' and 'M7' classes were used, followed by the 'N'class 2-6-0s and finally the 'West Countries'. None of these had any of the features such as small wheels which are often said to be necessary on steep gradients.

There was another party with its eye on Ilfracombe: the Great Western. Its long, rambling branch from Norton Fitzwarren to Barnstaple (Victoria Road) was in business by 1873. Although in various other places where the two met up the LSWR had to inveigle treaties out of the GWR, here the tyre was on the other wheel. The GWR had put its support behind a rival line which was turned down by Parliament, so it had to negotiate with the LSWR and in 1887 built a link line from its terminus to the Junction, enabling it to run trains to Ilfracombe from Taunton and beyond. Co-operation was excellent, and it was normal to see engines of one company hauling coaches or wagons of the other, or the two working together. From 1910 a traffic pooling agreement

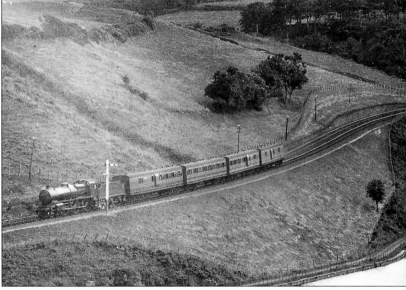

Above:
'M7' class 0-4-4T No 34, built at Nine Elms in April 1898, climbing the Slade Valley past the lower reservoir. As an example of inter-company co-operation, she is hauling a pair of Great Western coaches. The gradient of 1 in 36 is steep enough to be felt when walking it. *F. E. Box/IAL*

Right:
Going down the bank, a train of Warner coaches behind an 'N' class 2-6-0, then new in the late 1920s. The distant signal is one showing a permanent Caution/yellow light to remind the driver where he is. *F. E. Box/IAL*

operated, which meant that the receipts were divided according to a formula and it did not matter whose man booked the travellers or whose engine pulled them. Because it had no engine facilities west of Taunton, the GWR had to use tender engines of its intermediate 2-4-0 type, then after 1911 the '4300' class 2-6-0.

To carry this extra traffic the line was doubled between Pottington and Ilfracombe. It took three years to complete, rather longer than the time taken to construct the original railway. Ironically, this line had no provision for doubling, so extra land was needed and all the bridges had to be replaced, whereas almost all

Left:
Barnstaple Town station in 1931, with the main line on the right and the Lynton & Barnstaple on the left. The loop with the solitary wagon on it was seldom used for passing purposes, as the single-line section was only three-quarters of a mile long. The tall chimney is that of the Corporation's electricity generating station. In the distance are the Taw bridges and, on the other side, the buildings of Shapland & Petters. *L&G*

Centre left:
At Ilfracombe in 1928, digging into the promontory known as 'The Cairn', to make room for a new turntable and engine shed. In the far left, beyond the two-arm signal, wagons are being emptied where the carriage sidings are being extended. In line with the rock-face is the goods shed, and the old engine shed is partly visible behind it. *EWJC*

Below left:
An improvement at Ilfracombe in 1892 was this shelter to protect passengers from the sea breeze as they walked past the end of their train on their way out. It was made of timber. In this view it is nearly finished; inside it men are shaping canopy valance pieces and a painter is at work, on a ladder stood on the platform. The horse probably earned its keep hauling materials up from the town. *E. J. C. Daniell*

Above:
A view towards Braunton station, looking north from Braunton Gates level crossing. The station house is the large building to the left, the goods yard is to the right. Close on the left are two short sidings, generally used to park the banking engines. *LGRP/NRM*

Below:
August 1946; Barnstaple's river frontage, from Queen Anne's Walk to the Regal Cinema, with No 21C102 *Salisbury* coming over the bridge. Even the fervent railway enthusiast must admit that, as contribution to the scene, the bridge is more utilitarian than ornamental. *P. C. Short*

Left:
In the Upper Slade Valley, the
1.27pm through train from
Taunton descends the bank to
Ilfracombe. The engine is GWR
2-6-0 No 5336 and the leading
coach is a GWR Hawksworth
corridor brake third. *S. C. Nash*

the rest of the 'Withered Arm' had
accommodation for double track which was
never used. The section along the waterfront at
Barnstaple and over the river bridges remained
a single track. Even that the local authorities
considered an intrusion and prohibited any
widening.

Two further phases of improvement followed.
When the Lynton & Barnstaple Railway was
built in 1898 the platform at the north end of the
bridge called Barnstaple Quay was replaced by a
new station called Barnstaple Town. The site was
so cramped that it still had only one platform
and if you had tried to get out of a vehicle on the
crossing loop you would have gone straight into
the river. In 1928 the Southern Railway took
spades to Ilfracombe, dug a large hole at the
landward end, in which it placed a turntable for
the new larger engines coming into service, and
used the arisings to level the site for more
sidings.

Prior to 1914 the Torrington line was defined
as the main route from Barnstaple Junction. As
the holiday trade built up, Ilfracombe came to
fare rather better and from 1925 it was
designated the main line. Indeed, it was now
more valuable than Plymouth, which makes it
all the more inexplicable that nothing was done
to improve the line from Crediton to Barnstaple.
In the 1930s and again in the 1950s it had eight
trains from Waterloo alone on a summer

Saturday. The goods engine, which in winter
spent the weekend at the back of Barnstaple's
engine shed, would be found up the Mortehoe
Bank shoving away at them. The extra sidings
were then put to good use, extra engines came
down from Exmouth Junction, staff worked
overtime and seasonal labourers were taken on.

Physically, the area has some resemblance to
Torquay, and its lack of comparable growth has
been blamed on the later completion of its
railway. But although the beaches are
magnificent, they are frequently swept by
northwest winds never felt in Tor Bay. Also, the
running time from Exeter was typically 1hr
50min, against just over an hour to Torquay. The
best time ever achieved from Waterloo was 5hr,
and from Paddington it was a good half-hour
longer. Visitors to the area preferred it that way
as they preferred peace and quiet to crowds and
candyfloss, while the inhabitants regarded South
Devon as a vulgar place that had sold its soul to
the tourist trade. Only later did they change to
demanding easy movement, and then of course
what they demanded was roads.

The descent to Ilfracombe station, with
apparently nothing between the end of the line
and the sea far below, was one of the most
fearsome pieces of railway anywhere, but there
was only one instance of a train being unable to
stop at the bottom. This was the Locomotive
Superintendent Dugald Drummond's private

saloon car, which had inadequate brakes. Fortunately it was halted by contact with the buffer stops and only dignity was injured. Orders were that all trains weighing more than 180 tons had to include two brake vans or equivalents; speed was restricted to 25mph and all freight trains in either direction stopped at Mortehoe for the staff to put on all the wagon hand brakes.

Apart from its shape, the line had two significant handicaps. There were 11 road level crossings, and Government regulations laid down that each must have an attendant and be protected by gates and signals. The wages bill made the finances look bad, especially in winter. Down in Barnstaple, the Taw Bridge was a prominent object which annoyed the tourism interest in the Council. To them, railways were necessary evils, expected to deliver the tourists and then make themselves scarce. But here the bridge was, in its iron-girder muddiness, obstructing the river frontage, spoiling the view and lowering the tone. Its final removal was heartily welcomed.

Right:
This scene is on 4 July 1964, but it could have taken place at any time after 1928. A through train from Taunton comes down the bank, the fireman looking out while the driver handles the brake, which he cannot reach while looking over the side. From here we are looking through the engine shed. The signalbox is of the standard LSWR design, characterised by two sets of windows with a central brick pillar. The engine is 2-6-0 No 7306, built in 1921, and the coaches are BR Standards. *K. A. Stone/EWJC*

Below right:
'M7' No 670 tackles the 1 in 40 climb from Heddon Mill to the Hunters Inn with a Maunsell open third and a Bulleid composite coach. The date is 1 July 1950, but the engine, built at Nine Elms in October 1897, is still in Southern livery. The Maunsell coach, built in about 1935, is in new BR red and cream livery, and the Bulleid coach, built in about 1947, is in Southern green.
P. C. Short

Left:
This little engine, built by
W. G. Bagnall Ltd of Stafford,
was used by the contractor
James Nuttall in the
construction of the line. *L&G*

Centre left:
A view in Southern days at
Pilton depot. The driver of *Yeo*
finishes his oiling before
running down to the station. To
the right of the engine is a coal
stage with crane, and beyond it
a turntable, which was seldom
used as the engines always
faced north. There is a two-
road engine shed, a single-road
carriage shed and a two-road
carriage shed. *F. E. Box/IAL*

Below left:
Beside the carriage shed was a
goods station with a shed and
two sidings. This view shows
the full range of the railway's
wagon stock. *L&G*

Right:
The Lynton & Barnstaple had a
picturesque quality that can
only be assessed as un-English,
which added to its appeal for
holidaymakers. This view was
issued as a postcard by Frith
Bros. It shows a southbound
train entering Barbrook Woods
half a mile from Lynton. *EWJC*

6. Lynton & Barnstaple

The Lynton & Barnstaple Railway was an heroic enterprise of the kind the Englishman loves to contemplate — so long as he is not required to give it any actual support. With its grand scenery, excellent construction, complete equipment, quaint stations and adorable trains, it was the perfect narrow-gauge railway; too perfect for this world.

It was a local venture intended to provide a link to the outside world for the adjacent villages of Lynton and Lynmouth, which were sandwiched between the sea and the heights of Exmoor, over 20 miles from the nearest town. It did not apparently occur to the proprietors that the mountainous terrain, unpopulated country and quaint hamlets which made the area so unspoilt a retreat for the tourist also made it in the highest degree unlikely to generate enough business for a profitable railway.

The country presented obstacles enough even for the construction of a railway; but at this time the Ffestiniog Railway was at the height of its fame as an example of how railways could succeed in such terrain, so the promoters chose the same track gauge as that line, 1ft 11⅝in. A company was incorporated in June 1895 and the railway opened on 11 May 1898.

The line cost twice the estimated amount to build, which nowadays would be considered pretty good going but was then disastrous — it bankrupted the contractor. It was a full-size railway in everything but the gauge, and everything was done properly. Six stations were built with elegant buildings, staff houses and full signalling, and a well-equipped workshop was set up by the Pilton road, on the edge of Barnstaple. Where the line met the standard-gauge Ilfracombe line on the riverside the

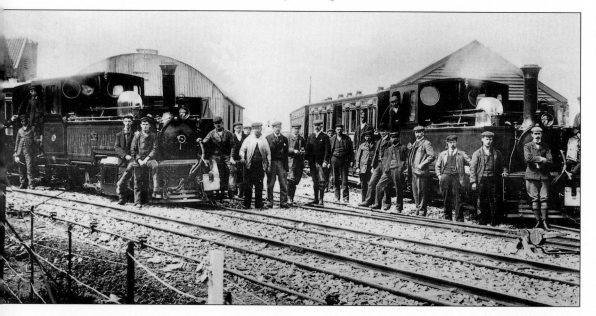

LSWR built a new station, called Barnstaple Town, which replaced the original platform at Barnstaple Quay. Unfortunately, the other stations were far less usefully situated. Chelfham, near the hamlet of that name, is remembered chiefly for its viaduct crossing a tributary of the River Yeo. Bratton Fleming, the largest place on the route, had a station half-a-mile distant, down a hill, which would seem negligible to the residents of a village whose top lay some 300ft above its lower end. Blackmoor Gate was a hotel at the top of the climb from Barnstaple and also the summit of the Barnstaple-Lynton road. Woody Bay station, named after a cove on the coast nearly three miles away which the railway hoped would become a resort, was at the other end of the summit section, by the Moorland Hotel at Martinhoe Cross. Lynton terminus was on a hillside 250ft above the village and 700ft above Lynmouth; 1 in 50 gradients and snaking curves were the rule.

From its Barnstaple terminus the line curved round beside the River Yeo, on the opposite side from Rolle Quay, and had its own siding and wharf for the import of coal. It crossed the Braunton and Pilton roads on the level. Then it followed the River Yeo, which it crossed several times, to the hamlet of Snapper, where there was a halt. Here the climbing started. Beyond

Chelfham it left the Yeo and continued up to Bratton Fleming on the edge of Exmoor, in a repeated succession of cutting, S-bend and embankment as it crossed each stream. Into the wild moorland scenery, it wound around the village of Parracombe in a multiple curve similar to that on the Ffestiniog Railway at Tan-y-Bwlch. Gaining the watershed, the highest point on the line, 980ft, was just to the east of Woody Bay station. There was a continuous descent at 1 in 50 from there, above the West Lyn River to Lynton terminus.

The railway bought 16 bogie coaches of the most modern type and 22 wagons from the Bristol Carriage & Wagon Co, and had another coach built by Shapland & Petter in Barnstaple. They were hauled by three 2-6-2T type engines supplied by Manning, Wardle & Co, named *Yeo*, *Exe* and *Taw*. These machines looked as if they had been designed to meet the classic image of a toy train, with tall thin chimneys, massive projecting couplings, boilers concealed in a box-shaped tank assembly and big cabs for the out-of-scale drivers. However, they weighed 22 tons and took four bogie coaches up that very heavy road. In 1900 the company bought another engine from the US firm of Baldwin. She was of similar size, but was a 2-4-2T built in the US style with such features as bar frames and compensated suspension, and was named *Lyn*.

Left:
Opening day, 11 May 1898. The staff assembled in Pilton depot, with *Yeo* and *Exe* and their trains and crews at the ready. *LGRP/NRM*

Right:
A southbound train at Bratton Fleming in the early years. Platforms were not thought necessary, but the signalman had a walkway of old sleepers to stand on while changing tablets, and, lying by the post, a snuffer for extinguishing the station lamps. *L&G*

Centre right:
L&B coach No 9. This was an observation car of a sort, with an open-sided compartment in the centre, which you entered through narrow doors from the adjoining compartments. It seated 50 passengers in a length of 39½ft, which compares favourably with standard-gauge vehicles.
L&G

Below right:
Eight-ton van No 23, the only L&B vehicle with a wooden underframe. It was built at Pilton in 1908. *L&G*

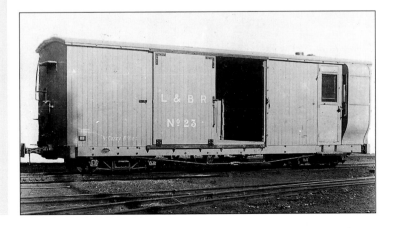

Left:
Two of the L&B wagons on the siding at Woody Bay station. They appear empty, but the wagon by the goods shed in the background is loaded with coal. The wagons were vacuum-fitted for safe working on the steep gradients and to enable mixed trains to operate. *LGRP/NRM*

Below:
This L&B train, heading north from Bratton Fleming, is mixed, with a wagon behind the engine. Taken on an unrecorded date during the Southern era. *LGRP/NRM*

The principal shareholder was Sir George Newnes, a publisher, and he bought two motor-omnibuses to ply the road (now the A339) between Blackmoor Gate station and Ilfracombe. This was the world's first railway feeder bus service. Local opposition was such that the police force was engaged to harass the vehicles and was soon able to prosecute one of the drivers for speeding. Sir George then sold the buses to the Great Western Railway, which used them for a similar service operating from Helston station to Lizard Town.

With the completion of the LBR, Barnstaple became quite a railway centre, with lines heading from it in five directions. This enhanced its status as the most important town in North Devon.

The LBR brought immediate benefits to its area; people could travel to Barnstaple and beyond, and the necessities of life became more available and cheaper. But for itself, it came nowhere near meeting the financial hopes of its owners. When the Grouping of the major railways was enacted by the Government in 1921 it was decided that what was good for big railways was good for little ones, so the company was wound up and the line sold to the new Southern Railway.

The Southern most obligingly spent a lot of its money on improvements to the railway. It relaid track, overhauled coaches and had eight new wagons built by J. & F. Howard of Bedford. It bought a new Manning Wardle engine to the original design, No 188 *Lew*. (The others were numbered 759, 760, 761 and 762 respectively.) This investment proved totally fruitless. The trains retained their toy-like aspect and

Right:
Showing off *Yeo* at Pilton in February 1928. The fireman has been using fire-irons to ensure that his fire is perfectly clean, always a problem on miniature engines. When built, the slide-bars were enclosed in a protective casing with a hinged access flap, but the flap was soon removed. The driver is in standard South Western garb, and his clogs are as polished as his engine. *F. E. Box/IAL*

Below right:
The Baldwin, *Lyn*, showing some of her US design features. This view was taken at Lynton, after 1907 when her boiler was replaced (which does not say much for the original, if it only lasted seven years).
A. R. Kingdom/EWJC

Left:
At the back of the shed was a small workshop. All repairs up to heavy overhauls were carried out here. L&G

delighted holidaymakers, but local people ignored them as soon as motor vehicles became reasonably dependable. Finding the service used for only a few weeks every year, the Southern decided to close it down. A public meeting was held in Barnstaple in the spring of 1935, but the case of those who protested against the closure collapsed when they had to admit that they had travelled to the meeting by car. The line closed without more ado on 29 September 1935 and the assets were promptly scrapped. The only surviving relics of any size remaining on site were the station houses, which became private dwellings, and the viaduct at Chelfham, which was left standing. All the rolling stock was destroyed on the spot except for *Lew*, sold to a dealer and

exported, and two coaches; No 2 was used as a summerhouse and was acquired in 1982 by the York Railway Museum, and No 15 was left on the line at Snapper Halt, whence the remains were removed many years later and used by the Ffestiniog Railway in an extensive rebuild.

When, in the 1950s, railway enthusiasts proved that a narrow-gauge line could be revived by voluntary effort, thoughts turned to the LBR. However, there was no original equipment to preserve and its land had been sold back to the farms, its road crossings restored to the highway authority and its buildings were all in use by new owners. None of these bodies was interested in giving up its property to someone's hobby. Even had it survived intact until the postwar years, its presence in Barnstaple town with level crossings over the two roads leading out to the northwest would certainly have been expunged. As a pure tourist attraction, it would have been proscribed on the grounds of bringing more cars into an area with bad roads. Short-lived, doomed by its own success, killed by the community that brought it into being, this was a railway just too romantic to survive.

Left:
Showing the engine and carriage sheds, with one of the Manning Wardles raising steam, *Lyn* indoors and carriage cleaning in progress. Photographs at Pilton were generally taken in the morning, when the sun was in the front of the buildings. *L&G*

Above right:
The railway's biggest and best known engineering work was Chelfham Viaduct. It is seen from the west in 1906, before the trees which came to dominate the area had grown up. *L&G*

Right::
A view from Chelfham station over the viaduct, possibly from the observation window at the rear of a northbound train, on a wet day. A siding was provided on the down side. *L&G*

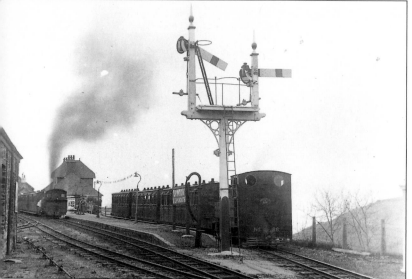

Above:
Parracombe, one of the larger villages near the route, was not given a station but just this halt. A supply of good water was available here, so trains generally stopped to water the engine from the tank standing in front of the road bridge. *L&G*

Centre left:
Lynton station lay high on the hillside above the village, a site chosen to minimise its impact on the scenery — and hence also its convenience to regular users. On a busy day, *Lyn* starts away while *Lew* waits for a later path. *LPC*

Below left:
The driver of *Exe* has a check round during the pause at Blackmoor Gate. As built, the engines had the cab front set in behind the front edge of the sides and roof. This recess scooped up exhaust steam very effectively. The leading van in this train is No 6, one of those built by Bristol Carriage & Wagon Co for the opening. *L&G*

Above:
Lynton terminus, looking towards the goods shed.
The station house would have enhanced a main-line
establishment; it was built by the principal local civil
engineers, Jones of Lynton, who put up similar
houses at Woody Bay and Blackmoor Gate. The pile
of cases and trunks on the platform is typical of
travellers' luggage in those days.
G. N. Southerden/EWJC

Below:
Barnstaple Town station, new and unsullied in 1898.
As might be expected, the building of a station on
the riverfront aroused the ire of the municipal
authorities. The L&B track was worked from a
proper signalbox; rodding may be seen running to
the points at the far end. The near turnout leads to a
transfer platform with the standard gauge.
F. E. Box/IAL

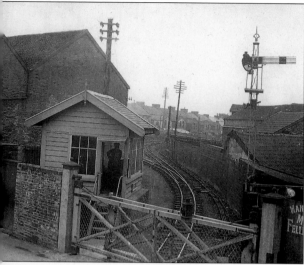

Left:
The level crossing gates at Pilton Road, at the south end of Pilton depot, which lies out of sight on the left. The crossing had four gates which overlapped when closed over the railway.
G. N. Southerden/EWJC

Below left:
The L&B was fitted up with signalling, using full-size equipment which loomed incongruously over the half-size track; as is shown by this view of the signals at Lynton controlling movement to and from the two platform lines. It was taken fairly early in the morning. *G. N. Southerden/EWJC*

Below:
A view south over Braunton Road level crossing towards the Taw and the Town station, whose signalbox is visible. *G. N. Southerden/EWJC*

Above:
Yeo waits to leave Lynton, while the guard sees a last passenger aboard. The engine driver has opened his regulator to warm the cylinders before starting. This was taken in the 1920s, when she carried a numberplate but had not been painted into Southern colours. *G. N. Southerden/EWJC*

Below:
A blurred but historically interesting view, taken from an L&B train, across the River Yeo to Rolle Quay, with typical coastal cargo ships and standard gauge wagons. *F. E. Box/IAL*

7. North Devon & Cornwall Junction

The countryside to the north of Dartmoor, valued by 20th-century holidaymakers for its peace and quiet, was in the 19th century a vibrant community: busy with farming, fishing, quarrying and mining. At the turn of the century the collapse of the mining industry and falling agricultural prices plunged the region into appalling poverty. This was the sort of situation at which the Light Railway Act of 1896 was aimed, and numerous railway schemes were proposed for this part of the southwestern peninsula. Only one was actually built.

The North Devon & Cornwall Junction Light Railway was formed with the intention of rebuilding the private Marland Clay Works narrow-gauge railway into a full-size public line and extending it south to Hatherleigh and west to meet the Bude branch at Halwill. It did not have anything to do with Cornwall. The company was founded in the year 1909 but did not obtain its Order until 1914, and, owing to the war, did not start construction until 1922. It was opened in its new form on 27 July 1925. The narrow-gauge main line between Torrington and Merton Moors was abandoned, although a couple of miles at the southern end was not converted and operations on the 3ft gauge around the quarries continued until 1971. Standard-gauge sidings were put in to the

Below:
Before the NDCJR, the Marland railway viaduct over the Torridge and the course of the Rolle Canal, now a road. *Photocrom Co/EWJC*

Marland works and to a loading plant near Meeth.

As engineer the company obtained the services of 'Mr Light Railway', Colonel Holman F. Stephens. The works were rather more substantial than on other projects of his, with neat stone-built stations equipped with platforms. Immediately south of Torrington station, the Marland railway crossed the River Torridge and the meadows on its south side by means of a marvellous timber viaduct which looked like the setting for a Wild West railway film. It was replaced by a conventional structure of steel spans on stone piers. From the end of it the line climbed into the hills on gradients as steep as 1 in 45 to a summit at Yarde, then down into the valley of the River Mere where the clay works lay. At the other end of the valley it crossed a ridge to rejoin the River Torridge. That enabled it to get near Hatherleigh — though not near enough — then it was uphill all the way to the moorland fastness of Halwill Junction.

Stations were provided somewhere near Petrockstowe (incidentally, 'Padstow' is 'Petrockstowe' contracted by greater use), Hatherleigh and Black Torrington, called Hole, and road-crossing halts at Watergate, Yarde, Dunsbear and Meeth. Although defined as a 'light' railway, it could accommodate full-size rolling stock and main-line locomotives, more

than could be said for some main lines. On at least one occasion, during the winter of 1946-7, when the all-important 'Atlantic Coast Express' could not get out over its usual route from Halwill to Okehampton because of snow, it was taken round by Torrington.

As it was built after the 1921 Railways Act, the NDCJR was not 'Grouped' into the Southern Railway. The managers of the latter may have thought that it was already too late for new lines — it was the last new full-size railway built in England (excepting reconstructions of existing routes). The economic decline of the surrounding countryside was persisting, and the Government initiative which brought it into being had been replaced by a policy of building roads and encouraging road haulage. Whatever the cause, the SR viewed it with a marked lack of interest and declined to take it over, although it was obliged to undertake its working. It did so in the manner of an aristocrat running an almshouse.

For a start, it was decreed that the line would be run as a unit. No through services, and no portions of London expresses. Freight, which was taken out via Torrington, was remarshalled, re-engined and altogether retarded at that place. Passenger trains also ran from Torrington, three a day right through and one to Petrockstowe and back. At Halwill Junction they were not even allowed into the

Above:
The only 'modern' element in this view of Hatherleigh station is the locomotive; an LMS-type 2-6-2T taking water on 1 July 1964. This was the only watering point on the line. *K. A. Stone/EWJC*

Right:
A view of Hatherleigh in 1931, showing two wagons in the yard. The station saw few passengers, being a mile from the town along the road seen in the distance, but it was an important distribution centre for fertiliser, produce and livestock. A stationmaster, who covered the whole line, was based here. *L&G*

station. A platform disguised as a pile of gravel was constructed off the end on the up side, where the NDCJR train was allowed to sit in the hope that some passengers might eventually find it.

To work this pariah of railways the Southern at first thought of buying some more of the Hawthorn Leslie engines it had on the Bere Alston & Callington. However, the Chief Mechanical Engineer R. E. L. Maunsell proposed using engines made redundant by electrification in the London area. The type selected was the LBSCR 'E1' 0-6-0T dating from 1874; designed for shunting, it was adapted for road service by enlarging the coal bunker, extending the frames and adding a trailing radial axle. Ten were converted, of which at any one time half were based at Barnstaple shed and half were kept at Exmouth Junction, where they were found useful for trip goods and banking on the St

David's-Central Incline. Later, Plymouth shed used a couple to take the place of the Callington Hawthorn Leslies.

Clay and cattle were the staples of the NDCJR. Passengers were rare sightings; not surprisingly, since in 1925 this was the poorest part of the whole southern half of England and by 1965 the population had fallen by a quarter. Patronage rose at first until by 1929 there were seven trains a day, but then buses swept the business up and from then on the outward bookings averaged three per train. Photographers made great play of being the only passenger on board and the train crew waiting for them to take their pictures; not realising the harm they were doing. The result was that the line gained a reputation of being the example of the useless railway, serving no purpose other than to waste taxpayers' money. Here, as in many places, if the railway had advertised its freight timetables to the public as well as its passenger services, its contribution to the community might have been better appreciated.

Funnily enough, this bucolic joke of a railway had the last laugh. It outlasted the Ilfracombe, Bude, North Cornwall, Turnchapel, Callington and Okehampton-Bere Alston lines by a good number of years.

Left:
Watergate Halt nestled among the trees by Watergate Bridge on the road up to Taddiport and Torrington. The level crossing was never gated. The timber was grown commercially. Seen on 15 August 1966. *B. Quemby*

Below:
Hole (for Black Torrington) was the same as Petrockstowe and a mirror image of Hatherleigh. Here, as at all the stations, the points and signals were worked by a small ground frame. *L&G*

Right:
The 'E1(R)' class was created especially for the NDCJR and 10 entered service over two years from May 1927. No 2124, built as LBSCR No 124 in 1878, is seen at Barnstaple depot in 1948. *RPC*

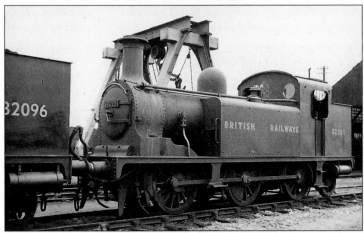

Centre right:
At Barnstaple shed on 20 June 1949, Nos 2095 and 2096. The gantry crane enabled the fitters to lift engines to deal with hot axleboxes. *S. C. Nash*

Below:
No 32610 on a typical passenger train, the 3.55pm Torrington-Halwill on 20 June 1949. The fireman relaxes during the stop at Hatherleigh. This 'E1(R)' was originally No 99, but from 1909 to 1922 was used exclusively to shunt Brighton locomotive depot, under the name *Locomotive Department*.
S. C. Nash

No wonder the stations were impeccably neat — the staff had nothing to do except tidy them. But it is unfair to blame the railway for the fact that you cannot force people to use the facilities you provide for them. Petrockstowe, 29 August 1963. *K. A. Stone/EWJC*

Acknowledgements

The existence of many of the photographs in these pages is a result of the work of Ian Allan Publishing, who collected and preserved material from some of the prewar photographers and companies — material which would otherwise have been destroyed in the era of philistinism. I am also grateful to another railwayman and enthusiast, Ted Crawforth. Other photographers' work is acknowledged, particularly Sid Nash. Some pictures were supplied by the National Railway Museum, York.

Origins of the prints used are designated as follows:

L&G	— Locomotive & General Railway Photographs
LPC	— Locomotive Publishing Co
RPC	— Real Photographs Co
IAL	— Ian Allan Publishing Library Collection
EWJC	— E. W. J. Crawforth Collection
NRM	— National Railway Museum

Bibliography

We are indebted to the authors of the many books on the subject, who between them have given us the history of these fascinating railways:

Black's Guide to Devonshire
Locomotives of the LSWR, D. L. Bradley, RCTS
The Wenford Mineral Line, Charles E. Lee, Railway Magazine
Portrait of the Lynton & Barnstaple Railway, Chris Leigh, Ian Allan Publishing
The Barnstaple & Ilfracombe Railway, Jim Lock, NDRPS
Branch Lines to Torrington, Vic Mitchell and Keith Smith, Middleton Press
The North Devon Railway, John Nicholas
The Bude Branch, David Wroe, Kingfisher
An Illustrated History of the North Cornwall Railway, David Wroe, Irwell
The London & South Western Railway, R. A. Williams, David & Charles